Deleuze and Gender
Deleuze Studies Volume 2: 2008 (supplement)

Edited by Claire Colebrook and Jami Weinstein

Edinburgh University Press

© Edinburgh University Press Ltd, 2008

Transferred to Digital Print on Demand 2011

Edinburgh University Press Ltd
22 George Square, Edinburgh EH8 9LF

Typeset in Sabon
by SR Nova Pvt Ltd, Bangalore, India

A CIP record for this book is available from the British Library

ISBN 978 0 7486 3892 5

The right of the contributors
to be identified as authors of this work
has been asserted in accordance with
the Copyright, Designs and Patents Act 1988.

Contents

Reviews

Introduction Part I

Claire Colebrook   University of Edinburgh

Could there, today, be such a person or persona as a feminist philosopher? We ask this question with two motifs in mind: the first is Deleuze and Guattari's notion of the conceptual persona, where philosophical theories are constituted through the co-production of certain characters (Deleuze and Guattari 1994), and the second is the notion of an internal pragmatism as articulated in *Difference and Repetition* (1994). It is now time to direct these questions – of the persona (which is internal to a text) and the vectors created by a text – to the Deleuzian corpus. Following not only *What is Philosophy?*, where Deleuze and Guattari argue that the production of a philosophical plane and its conceptual movements are accompanied by personae, but also *Nietzsche and Philosophy*, where Deleuze argues that the forces of texts are modes of *dramatis personae*, we might ask about the style of life that accompanies Deleuze's thought. It is that tortured concept of 'becoming-woman' that raises the question of the value of a concept, and its relation to the voice responsible for its articulation.

One possible way of answering this question would be to suggest that if Deleuze aimed at thought 'without an image' (Deleuze 1994: 208) or a becoming-imperceptible (Deleuze and Guattari 1987: 279), then – despite what Deleuze and Guattari say in *What is Philosophy?* about philosophy and personae – their own work might be one of the first moments in the history of philosophy where concepts are created without personae. That is, if all thinking up to the present has presupposed the good will of a thinker, and if this thinker has been a version of man (as the assumed standard from which others deviate) then becoming-woman would be a depersonalisation, a liberation from personification, images of thought and the notion that there are thinkers first, and then the concepts they use as tools or supplementary methods (Deleuze and Guattari 1987: 376). But there is an alternative, and that is to see a distinction between the subject of enunciation, who precedes and grounds judgment, and the persona (especially the persona that would accompany 'becoming-woman'). Becoming-woman would be crucial to the dissolution of the subject, and to thinking of texts, ideas and concepts not as *tools* (where a thinker uses a concept for certain ends, according to whether they work) but as weapons: something thrown or projected that expends force but without a determined production (Deleuze and Guattari 1987: 287). It is in this regard that Deleuze and Guattari align becoming-woman with the 'war machine': not an actualised war, such as philosophical or 'theory' wars with opposition among combatants, but a war of forces without underlying terms (Deleuze and Guattari 1987: 278). It is always possible to see feminism as war: as a group attack on patriarchy where there would be subjects who would then need to find the best conceptual resources. In such cases war as an object would be an accident or supplement (Deleuze and Guattari 1987: 418); actual wars would appear to be deviant or parasitic. A war on men or masculinity (even a war on war) would be a justifiable temporary violence oriented to a state beyond conflict.

But Deleuze and Guattari argue that this apparent supplement or accident, or the actual occurrence of wars, indicates a war-machine that, far from being alien to rational man and humanism, enables his existence, *and* provides a means of thinking his escape. Referring to Derrida in their notion of the logic of the supplement, they insist that what appears to be an accident or an addition to the man of reason – wars, combats battles – is actually evidence of a war in general, or a war machine. It is this 'war machine' that allows something like a State, and the accompanying form of the good thinker of common sense to be formed, for the State harnesses forces and relations into organised bodies of combat. It also has its own epistemology, for by placing war as an object to be used *by men*, the State creates the idea that war is an accidental occurrence for the sake of a greater good. If, however, man and war, or the relations of bodies in combat, are the effects of a war-machine, then this would have three consequences.

First, that which we take to be the norm and ground – the man of common sense and good will oriented to peace who fights a war in order to win over others to the truth that he has discerned – covers over the war machine of life; it precludes a perception of the forces from which we are composed, the forces that create relations and the powers that thought may be able to engage. Second, this epistemology has a sexual character, again given in the structure of man as a thinking organism. (This is spelled out in Deleuze's and Guattari's theory of the oedipality of the secret.) It is from the hysteria of the child, a child who perceives a secret that is held apart and that constitutes his private being, that man 'evolves' to a position of virility. Here, there is no secret from which one has suffered or which sets one apart from the domain of communication; rather, there is only a structure *that there is a secret, that there is the hidden*, and it is this perception of a ground beyond perception and relations that produces a structure of paranoia. And again this could be aligned with a style of agonistics and a style of war: from Kant onwards it has been the absence of a capacity to know, an anti-foundationalism, that has resigned us to conclude that all we can have is an ongoing conversation oriented towards legitimation that never arrives (Habermas 1992). Third, it is this covering over of the war machine by a State of warring bodies, that indicates or intimates becoming-woman. If virile paranoia is structured by a sense of a lost, hidden and unknowable secret, then woman – who *is* the secret – occupies not one more place in the terrain, but a different style of terrain, and possibly a different mode of persona.

This is why, I would suggest, becoming-woman is a useless and paralysing concept if it is used within theory and within wars among theoretical personae. As an example we could consider the false battle of essentialism: *either* woman exists as a substance outside the way we think of the human (which would enable emancipation, liberation and change) *or* woman is an effect of the ways in which the human has been constructed and it is the idea of construction is such that is liberating – no more enslavement to essences. Not only has the terrain of feminism actually never been that simple, as evidenced by the amount of ink spilt over deciding whether Judith Butler does away with the body and sex or grants sex a power far more efficacious than mere biology; it is also the case that if feminism means anything, then it somehow has to intervene differently in the way in which battles are fought according to meaning. So, rather than define a battle according to whether woman does or does not exist, let us imagine something more *practical* in the the Kantian sense (or what Deleuze refers to as internal pragmatics). Given that we discern the war machine or the positive play of forces only among men who are structured by a paranoid virile form of secrecy – *that there is a hidden but we do not know it and so the battle goes on* – what would it be to occupy the position of a body for whom there is no secret, for whom there is no position within a warring paranoid terrain and whose possibility (if she were to speak) would create a persona that would not be in command of forces for the sake of some end of man?: 'Such is the form of exteriority, the relation between brother and sister, the becoming-woman of the thinker, the becoming-thought of the woman: the *Gemut* that refuses to be controlled, that forms a war machine' (Deleuze and Guattari 1987: 378).

To consider a form of feminism as becoming-woman, or as associated with the war machine, requires both the dissolution of subjects as external to, or before, pragmatics and the construction of conceptual personae. Becoming-woman is not in conflict with the persona of the feminist philosopher, for the feminist philosopher is not one who thinks, who thinks well, or who directs good thinking to the right ends. The feminist philosopher as conceptual persona, as moving with the war machine rather than war, would allow a new form of agonistics – not just another persona added to the history of philosophy, but a new style of philosophy. Such a possibility is not, I would suggest, a distant, utopian or impossible future but can already be intuited in the space of feminism as we know it today. Indeed, it is the rather embarrassing, awkward, appropriating tone of this horrible concept – becoming-woman – that paradoxically requires us to evaluate concepts differently. The concept is embarrassing when it closes down thinking: when it is left to feminist philosophers to disentangle this monstrous thread, while the real Deleuze philosophy and Deleuze studies gets on with the nuts and bolts of materialism. The embarrassment and awkwardness should not be seen as unfortunate or accidental: it cannot be explained away by accepting that Deleuze and Guattari were having a French moment when they made this appeal to becoming-woman, and that what we really require is a Deleuze studies that can go beneath such figures and metaphors to the real matter. But can we, should we ('we'?), allow this distinction to be maintained between a philosophy's mere form and the matter or system that can be adjudicated systematised, translated and liberated from its style? Again we face an awkwardness, because becoming-woman is articulated as *the* way to think matter differently, and to think matter a such.[1] For becoming-woman, and its association with both the war machine and a certain form of the secret, is a way of trying to arrive at 'materials-forces' (Deleuze and Guattari 1987: 329), where there is no matter outside variation, force, relation and difference: 'The secret has its origin in the war machine; it is the war machine and its becomings-woman, becomings-child, becomings-animal that bring the secret' (Deleuze and Guattari 1987: 287). There is not a matter that is then expressed in thinking, with various positions warring over materialism *or* idealism, Marxism *or* Freudianism, feminism *or* a post-feminist liberation from sexuality.

We might begin to see that it is this concept in Deleuze studies, the concept of becoming-woman, that has at once been the most destructive – precluding the smooth transition to an understanding of Deleuze – but which in its indigestibility offers us food for thought. This would not be the totem meal that consumes the father in order that the brothers might live on, battle on, and acknowledge that they have killed the ends of man only to arrive at a domain of communication. Rather, the taking-in of this concept of becoming-woman generates a new concept of dissonance, which is therefore a new structure of the war of thinking. One way of considering dissonance, or the incommensurability and war of opinions is through the masculine virile paranoid form: there is no truth outside the assertion, well-formedness and legitimation process of argument, so this entails a relation of ongoing battle among good thinkers. A rogue thinker – one who absented himself from conversation and claimed a fundamental intuition of the truth – would be the object of discipline, but all in the name of keeping the play of perspectives open (Rorty 1998). If, however, we adopt the practical potential of becoming-woman then the nature of the philosophical persona is quite different. If it is not the case that there is some hidden ground from which we are separated by virtue of our finitude but, on the contrary, there is matter and life only in expressions, noise and chatter *all of which express the infinite but from a singular point, with no point being in command of the whole*, then dissonance is not the failure of harmony, or a dissonance on its way to a harmony that never arrives (Deleuze 1993). Dissonance is the song of the earth as such. Becoming-woman is the most disastrous of concepts if considered as an object of war, where we could either decide that it is good or bad for feminism, or a minor moment in an otherwise serious corpus. The concept of becoming-woman creates embarrassment for the serious thinkers who need to leave it aside while granting women the right to a squabble regarding its efficacy. By pushing this disastrous embarrassment further, though, we might avoid the worst peace of perpetual management and begin to think those dissonances that take us beyond organic quiescence. Becoming-woman, as a concept with its attendant personae, is intrinsically opposed to the good will of the thinker, and it is for this reason that it has done violence to feminism and Deleuze studies.

In order to see how this is so let us ask this question: what would it mean to shut down this concept once and for all? Two possibilities: a philosopher demonstrates that 'becoming-woman' is pragmatic: we happen to confront a plane of thinking that has been organised according to sexual binaries, with man at the centre, but this is not essential. We begin with trying to think another figure, woman, and then move beyond figures (Lambert 2006). (The war is localised and temporary, and oriented to arriving at good sense, where sense is the sense of the true Deleuzian spirit and the right form of life.) Second possibility and one that I would suggest we begin to pursue: we do away with the notion of the inessential figure, the accident or cliche that befalls thought as if from outside. We regard the intrusion of this ugly concept into an otherwise respectable corpus not as an unfortunate lapse in rigour, nor as a throwing of a salvo to give women something to think about – pragmatically – while the boys get on with ontology. Rather, we begin to think the ways in which it is the very awkwardness of concepts that makes a philosophy possible – its creation and daring, and breaking free from figures – that will also do a twofold violence to the corpus.

As an example I would cite one of the earliest interventions in what was not yet 'Deleuze Studies.' In *Patterns of Dissonance* Rosi Braidotti (1991) argues for a feminist subject who would be a necessarily presupposed, positive and constructive persona. Her existence is neither prior to feminist questions nor a simple discursive and illusory effect of the performance of feminist interventions. In *Patterns of Dissonance* Braidotti was already posing Deleuzian style problems that took the risk of refusing what Manuel Delanda (2006) has berated as 'the linguistic paradigm': there is not only a tactical or strategic problem in denying the possibility of the subject of enunciation; there is also an ontological or vital problem. Life cannot be reduced to the systems or structures that are known and actualised, for there are potentialities or living tendencies that exist, insist and inflect that orders of discourse and action we negotiate. The feminist subject of *Patterns of Dissonance* is therefore best read, I would suggest, as a refusal of discursive or negative approaches (where subjects are nothing other than nodes of subjection, points of interpellation) and as a rejection of a pre-philosophical or *transcendent* empiricism where one simply posits what women literally are. Instead, it makes sense to see the feminist subject as a consequence of a transcendental empiricism: all we have is this one dynamic and dissonant life, with no overarching or unifying system of relations (empiricism), but this life that we live, feel and negotiate is always *more than* its actualised terms. The task of the transcendental (in *Patterns of Dissonance*) takes the form of the production of a feminist subject. This is a subject who is the positive potentiality to question, mobilise, become and *think* the desires and relations that subtend the array of discourses, or the patterns of dissonance that compose any philosophical or political terrain. So we might at one and the same time affirm the necessity of thinking of the feminist philosopher as conceptual persona: it is she who asks *whose* discourse, whose statement, whose subjection, performance, passion or negativity is expressed in this or that specific dissonance.

At the same time, as *feminist*, this persona is not a figure defined by its active predicates – the one who doubts, affirms, negates and arrives at certainty – but is in a pattern of dissonance. For a new persona is only possible if something occurs in a text that marks a threshold and requires a reorientation in thinking; awkwardness is essential if thinking is going to be more than the free flow of easy conversation, or the war of one body against another.

To attempt to state this awkwardness less awkwardly let us look at how this concept of becoming-woman has been evaluated in terms of external pragmatics. Two male philosophers create a concept that seems to give women a role not only in thinking, but in life as such, in a new theory of matter, perception and creativity. But herein lies just the problem: for it seems as though thinking, just at the moment when it wishes to express daring and becoming, falls back into an appeal to the feminine: not women, but 'something' that women, too, need to tap into (Jardine 1985). So perhaps, here, we need to overcome the external pragmatism of 'becoming-woman' – deciding whether 'we' accept or reject this concept, whether it should be justified or expunged – and think about becoming-woman in its most scandalous, least appealing and *stupid* potentiality. Rather than read Deleuze and Guattari theologically – aiming for the spirit of the text beneath the unfortunate French letter – we should take this concept of 'becoming-woman' as evidence (as if evidence were needed) that the matter of thinking always comes from elsewhere: from figures, cliches, and war zones that have organised prior battles of forces. This stupidity can be evaluated from the outside: here we would ask whether 'we' should still think in terms of man and woman? Alternatively, we can seize hold of this stupidity and refuse the exclusive disjunction of regarding 'becoming-woman' as *either* good or evil.

If thinking does not proceed from a good will, and if the forms of thought are not mediations of matter, then we might confront the benevolent stupidity and malevolent intelligence of the matter-expression of thinking. There is not a thinking that confronts matter as some object to be formed, nor a good thinking that follows from the proper development of matter. Against thought as the extension or evolution of a life oriented towards good sense and self-recognition, Deleuze and Guattari create the concept of becoming-woman to at least begin to *demoralise thinking*: both thought without a morality, and a thought that confronts its breakdown and absence of guarantee. This is not an 'on the one hand, on the other hand' logic (Deleuze 1994: 282), where we see that while we might need to begin with the idea of woman in its most cliched and stupid form (associated with secrecy, celerity, girlhood and birdsong) we would then need to move on and start thinking without such figures. Rather, becoming-woman is thought *and* unthought at one and the same time. It is matter expressing itself, with the human organism giving order to chaos by referring to sexed bodies as coded in the familial assemblage; at the same time it is an attempt to create a style of thinking that is not a correct representation so much as a style of provocation that has no external criteria.

Let us consider this broad-brush and possibly overly literal beginning of becoming-woman in terms of philosophical conceptual personae. The persona that follows from a philosophy of becoming-woman and becoming-imperceptible is a curious hybrid: Deleuze and Guattari warned against a complete or absolute deterritorialisation, and instead emphasised the creation, not dissolution, of masks and styles. They insisted on personae, or thought figures, rather than masters who would act as grounds for judging either the value of a text or its sense. When Deleuze argues for an 'internal pragmatiism' he suggests that we do not simply trace back a philosophy's force to its institutional and authorial proper names, but instead look at how modes of argument, concept-creation and problem-production effect ways of living. If a philosophy is excessively organised, or assumes a relation of powers narrowed to man as a speaking, rational, calculating and rule-following being, then the wide range of 'what a body can do' is domesticated by one of the body's functions.

We might note, today, with all the work undertaken on the body as an autopoetic unity geared towards its own equilibrium and homeostasis (Damasio 2003; Maturana and Varela 1987; Thompson 2007), that we are in the presence of a highly rigid plane, where the human organism is figured in a hysterically normative manner. Further, such an articulation occurs with a very clear conceptual persona of the philosopher as emancipator. We are, we are constantly told, suffering from centuries of flabby metaphysics and Cartesian images of mind as spirit; what we need to do is return to an accurate model of vital life, recognise man as a practical organism for whom thinking is an *extension* of life-sustaining movement, and regain a proper view of the world (Varela, Thompson and Rosch 1991). We undertake a global war on the lures of bad metaphors: mind as machine, mind as computer, mind as ghost in the machine or mind as separate substance (Flanagan 2007). The corrective for such stupidities is a theory of systemic life, thoroughly grounded in the organism and meaning. Man is now a self-maintaining bounded machine, and the world is nothing other than the milieu of potential responses according to man's ongoing, dynamic and responsive selfhood. One of the ways in which Deleuze has functioned as a proper name has been to consecrate a return to living systems, a rejection of any notion of mind or sense independent of living bodies. This appeal to vitalism functions, despite Deleuze and Guatari's insistence that their vitalism is technical and machinic, as a return to genetic life, life as genesis or unfolding.

When Deleuze has been *accused* of vitalism (rather than read with a nuanced sense of what vitalism might mean) it has been this aspect of supposed literalism that has been targeted (Hallward 2006). Against a Deleuzian return to 'life' as some monist flux beyond the entities of this world, Alain Badiou has asserted the subject *as function;* for it is only in the act outside calculation and the already enumerated that something like thought can occur (Badiou 2005). It is perhaps not surprising that Badiou appeals to the tradition of the radical subject, and that such an appeal has force: for the mantra of anti-Cartesianism that defines theory today has had the effect of retreating back into the primacy of the self as an organism. We are left with an exclusive disjunction: either we consider life in terms of organic systems, their milieux, and the always located meaning a body makes of its world, *or* we posit the subject as a potentiality to think. Such a subject would be nothing other than a break with, or negation of, organic plenitude. And it is here that we can see the beginnings of the force of the feminist conceptual persona. Theory today battles itself out among combatants: either Badiou *or* Deleuze, either Deleuze *or* a Deleuze modified by Derrida. This battle has an internal style, which we can discern in the constant use of diagnostics: either we lament the fall into Cartesianism that can be overcome by theories of life (Damasio 1994), or we lament philosophy's fall into poetry and regard it as redeemable only through a radically formal mathematics (Badiou 1999). And then there is that ragbag of lesser 'thinkers' known as feminists, who do not create systems in order to mark out a proper name as a terrain, but occupy and move with forces.

If Deleuze can be thought, today, with the concepts and figures he contributes – including 'becoming-woman' – it is in relation to a plane that has become rigidified around the opposition subject-organism. Either thinking and living is grounded in organic and meaningful life, with thought being an extension of self-maintaining processes (Hansen 2000) *or* we can posit subjects as negations of that constituted domain. Either Cartesian dualism or an organic monism (Zizek 1999). As an example of this type of plane, with its attendant persona, we need only think of the new anti-Cartesian man of cognitive science, who has broken away from metaphysics, and found himself in a new and manageable domain of systems theory. Defined against old models of centralised thinking, man is now stratified between his body as an equilibrium mechanism and a milieu that is given as always meaningful from the point of view of the organism (Thompson 2007). To think of Deleuze as a philosophical persona (as a possible figure for a different style of thinking, one that will confuse science and poetry, sexual figures and physical models) may release us from this highly gendered model. Deleuze regarded the attainment of the body without organs as the end of his philosophy of becoming: rather than maintain a balance among powers, or be oriented by the organs acting in concert to regulate one's external world, the 'body without organs' would extend sight to the point of thinking the invisible in the visible, the ear to hearing the sonorous in sound, and the brain to thinking beyond the given, the lived and the communicable.

Notoriously, Deleuze opposed the self-authoring man of philosophical systems – whose world and others would always be in accord with his own organic striving – with a violent production of philosophical progeny. To take a previous philosopher 'from behind' (Deleuze and Parnet 1987) would create a future of the philosophical text not anticipated in the original text's genesis. The Deleuzian persona is avowedly monstrous, neither a man of insemination giving form to a matter that awaits his potency, nor an oedipalised son striving to maintain and expand the proper legacy of the history of philosophy. True philosophical fidelity, being a true son of a philosophical father, requires bastardry: do not extend, but pervert those powers in a text that did not flow organically from a preceding good will. Read a text for its potential to expand rather than normalise the human organism. As an example of Deleuze's own reading we might think of Bergson's concept of pure perception, which is the intuition of the power to perceive liberated from the sensory motor complex of the specific speed of the human body. Despite Bergson's orientation in *The Two Sources of Morality and Religion* (1985) to arrive at a humanity that would extend the intellect to perceive spirit as such, Deleuze used the concept of intuition to create concepts of becoming-imperceptible: concepts that tend towards a liberation from the body perceived as self-bounded unity and towards a becoming of the world as such. As Rebecca Hill notes in this volume, Bersgon's philosophy harboured its internal stupidities, those moments when it defined thinking as such according to a limited and localised body of Western man. Perhaps that stupidity is overcome and intensified in becoming-woman, for this concept at once recognises just how imbricated the image of thought is with man as an organism, but in defining the passage beyond that as 'becoming-woman' takes an incalculable risk of cliche. Deleuzian concepts are those, then, that recognise minimal and supple degrees of stability, and work towards impersonality. The persona that attaches to this style of concept is not that of the good and upright thinker who precedes style, but a thought that creates a body through style, a body that perhaps is at odds with self-maintenance and life-furthering.

Certainly one would release such a philosophical persona from *gender*, for the philosopher could not be the man of insemination nor the woman of care and nurturance. This becoming liberates itself from the man oriented to good sense, common sense and the equilibrium of the faculties, beginning with at least one other style of perception and relation to the outside that has not been determined in advance by a norm of right reason. This raises the question, then, of what type of persona is enabled by the taking up of this becoming-woman, for Deleuze and Guattari suggest that the persona of becoming-woman is a persona on its way to becoming-imperceptible, moving away from a molar subject, which may be necessary but should only be a passage toward 'thought without an image.'

If the affect created by a certain form of literature can be called 'Dickensian,' 'Kafka-esque,' or 'Lawrentian' (where we refer neither to any specific character, nor any sentence or content so much as a mode of living one's milieu), then the concepts created by philosophers can be referred to as 'Kantian' – concepts that are formal, constructivist, transcendental – or Cartesian, in their commitment to dualism, foundation, clarity. The personae that attach to these concepts are not biographies, so much as the figure or character whose style of thinking would have unfolded a certain mode of problem: a doubting Descartes, an always questioning Kant, a cantankerous Schopenhauer. Could such personae be female or feminist? Luce Irigaray suggested that if such personae were to occur then the nature of philosophy would be altered radically, not just in a reconfiguration of the plane of all philosophical concepts (as Deleuze suggests, where each new name and concept creates a re-reading of the whole), but in a ground-shattering and almost affective re-ordering of the very orientation of thinking. We would not have, in Irigaray's feminist philosopher, a single persona but something like a couple. Irigaray suggests this in *I Love to You* (Irigaray 1996) where a sexually different persona would undertake questioning, proposing, doubting, affirming, remembering or disputing always in relation and conversation with an other who would, in turn, be both affected by and affective towards the address. Irigaray's philosophy created its own exegetical battles in the theory world – 'for and against essentialism' – even though the mode and style of her text, which spoke through the figures and tropes in philosophy showed the ways in which the logic of essence and accident occurred only through a certain agonistics and a certain relation to the outside. It is that relation to the outside that also marks Deleuze's commitment to life, and has perhaps lured us into a literal laziness, where becoming-woman appears as a stylistic tic rather than an necessary act of war the Deleuzian corpus took upon itself.

Now it is here, in this curious commitment to a theory of life, that we can find in Deleuze and Guattari a means of thinking personae beyond Deleuze's ambivalently virile image of 'taking a philosopher from behind.' Let us consider this figure in terms of philosophy's clichés and desires: if Platonism imagined the formative power as giving life to a chaotic matter, and if creative insemination is always master of itself because all emanations reflect and recognise their divine and grounding source, then Deleuze suggests a new sexual motif for creative time: not fathering through insemination, but a form of sterile and suggestively violent coupling resulting in bastard offspring that would seem to have no natural genesis. Elsewhere Deleuze (1990) refers to creations of sense as sterile, incorporeal and monstrous, often opposing violence to the man of common sense, and also aligning the war machine (and the man of war) with the feminine *against* majoritarian man. So let us pause to ask a tired old question: is becoming-woman in Deleuze and Guattari's philosophy a hackneyed gesture of reappropriation in which the speaking subject deploys an imagined fecund and extra-rational source in order to overcome his historical and emasculating rationalisation? Or, is this gesture towards becoming-woman an opening of thought, appealing to women not as they are, but as they might become once released from the normative binaries of bourgeois, capitalist, familial and productive norms? How might we decide such a question? The simple answer is through reading, but this then raises the question of how we read Deleuze: from behind, without due reverence, hoping not for fathered children but for monstrous ramifications? Or, is it more complex? Did Deleuze, because he wanted to tear Freud, Marx and others away from the familial and organic idea of man as a productive and self-maintaining body read these philosophers against their implicit theories of life (Freud's death drive, Marx's species being)? How then do we read Deleuze and Guattari's 'becoming-woman'? I would suggest that fidelity – explaining, justifying, condemning this concept as a lapse – remains within a highly theological mode of reading whereby a text is the material expression of a spirit, a spirit that should be maintained, consecrated and corrected in its surface detail according to its proper sense. But there are resources within Deleuze's own philosophy that allow us to read otherwise. Here, it would not be a question of identifying a figure, such as becoming-woman, and then negotiating how that serves a group of readers, or how it allows us to judge an author. Such a theological reading, that regards texts as vehicles that might be judged according to the proper intent of their origin and the proper unfolding of their consequences amounts to an external pragmatism, where we evaluate styles according to already constituted (in this case organic) bodies. Let us suggest another path, one that follows from the *problem* of Deleuze and feminism: problems can be well posed or badly formed, but are opportunities for creation and transformation.

Deleuze suggests that in addition to women as a constituted population, created in a territorial relation with men through a historical assemblage of families, literary figures, cultures of reproduction and modes of reading, there is also a becoming-woman in which the very capacities that create women as part of a territory potentially open out onto a new assemblage. So this would allow us to think not of changing women's status within an assemblage, nor of giving women more power, and certainly not of escaping power and arriving at a woman's being-in-itself before all relations. On the contrary, becoming-woman allows for a different mode of agonistics: not women taking on a different role, but transforming just what it is to play a role, what it is to form a territory, what it is to make sense, and therefore what it is to read. Reading should not be the disclosure of a hidden secret, the unveiling of a sense that is the causal ground for being; nor is reading a creation ex nihilo with no relation to the outside. In Deleuze's own figure, taking a philosopher from behind seems at once to extend a masculinism in philosophy that creates from itself with no relation to the other, at the same time as it acknowledges that reading is an encounter, but one that is not appropriately figured through conventional couplings of a fruitful marriage, conversation, reflection or discourse.

In A *Thousand Plateaus* Deleuze and Guattari make two manoeuvres that complicate a ready association between thought as productive insemination, and reading as disclosive fidelity, and in these two manouvres they refigure sexual difference through a twisted binary. The first manoeuvre is their sexualisation of the secret, which is the sexualisation of styles of question rather than bodies; the second manoeuvre is their suggestion of a 'war machine' beyond male-male combat. We can deal with these intertwining motifs in sequence before returning to the problem of the feminist persona, a problem that should alert us, today, to some of the risks of 'Deleuze studies.' For it is the idea that there is a secret to Deleuze, a sense held by a band of brothers who have killed the father of logocentrism, that is intrinsically sexual and comes ready-made with its own forms of combat: do we read Deleuze as a materialist, a spiritually-inclined vitalist, a proletarian-despising high modernist or the great sustainer of late Marxism? As I indicated earlier, Deleuze and Guattari describe a passage from the secret as hysterical childhood event (something that occurs that defines a content that cannot be given proper form of expression) to the secret as an infinite paranoid virile form: there is a secret but it has no content, and all we can do is be enslaved to a certain never-knowing, while regarding ourselves as the beings we are – man – just through this loss of knowledge. The 'secret' as infinite paranoid virile form structures a style of speaking, questioning, discoursing and proposing that can be studied, as Deleuze studies his own philosophers, according to an *internal pragmatics*: we do not, here, look at the institutions, contexts and bodies in order to assess the force and power of positions, but look at the ways styles of position create fields and modes of force. That is, if there is some ultimate hidden sense or genetic ground, then arguments would concern a transcendent term and combatants would evaluate each other to the extent to which they were more or less in accord with that norm. (Such a logic applies to certain feminist arguments: is 'becoming-woman' good or bad for women, us women, we women, the women we ought to become?) A certain mode of reading, a certain style of subject effected in relation to knowledge takes a 'paranoid virile form': there is a secret, a sense, a ground and origin; but not only can such a secret not be known or disclosed, all we are left with is a pure form – *that there is secrecy, that there is the hidden* – with no positive content outside our emasculated position of not knowing. We have passed, they suggest, from a childhood hysteria (whereby my being is marked by a secret event whose logic I play out but do not know) to an adult paranoia: there is nothing to be discovered, nothing to be disclosed, but we are all subjected, finite and diminished by an origin or past that is no less paralysing for being fictive. Another mode exists, which Deleuze and Guattari describe as becoming-woman: nothing is hidden, everything is transparent, and there is a high degree of chatter. Rather than relations among bodies being organised around a contested ground or privileged object, and rather than agonistics being determined by a norm outside relations (such as a contestation for women as the spoils of war), becoming-woman is allied both with the 'war machine' and a becoming-imperceptible of the secret.

The war machine is the play of forces not yet assembled into opposed bodies placed in a terrain; for terrains, bodies, positions and their identifying traits occur through the play of forces. Rather than functioning as a ground or criteria of ethics, the Idea of the war machine, and the concept of becoming-woman with which it is associated, aims at a new style of ethics: for it does not posit an outside or other of force and violence but regards actual wars, combats and the persons and positions of terrains as ways in which violence is managed. This brings us to the curious, and possibly unpalatable, connection between becoming-woman and a truly violent war machine that would oppose actualised wars. Becoming-woman is neither the occupation of a position nor the evaluation of strategies and forces from some actual or imagined ideal. The 'man of war' for Deleuze and Guattari is associated with becoming-woman and the 'feminine line' precisely because he flees from constituted political battles. This can be thought concretely, according to a logic in which Deleuze and Guattari can be seen to be offering a sober analysis. Their description of the State's appropriation of the war machine describes actual war as a *supplement*, or outcome of a necessary synthesis. War is not a separate accident, an aberration that occurs despite or against humanitarianism; there are actual wars – bodies in identifiable combat – because there is the war machine, forces irreducible to persons and interests. As a consequence every battle and war draws upon a violence it must manage, but that can also deviate from the identifiable rationalisations of the State. We could think here of the ways in which the military can only operate by training bodies to kill other identifiable bodies for certain causes and in certain domains, but that this State war always opens the risk that those same forces will deviate or create a line of flight from the legitimised battle. As the recent documentary on abu ghraib – *Standard Operating Procedure* – disclosed, the war on terror was also a highly sexualised fleeing from clearly demarcated and purposive battles, becoming a highly cliched erotic assemblage in which bodies were pictured, posed, placed into narrative scenes and accompanied by dynamics of desire that were at once typically hetero-normative (prisoners humiliated through sexual passification) but also evidence of a line of flight, beyond man as sovereign agent and active manager. But why see aberration as becoming-feminine, and what can it tell us about secrecy, reading, and internal pragmatics? To understand this I would suggest that the complex tying becoming-woman with the war machine and the feminine form of secrecy precludes sense and good judgment.

That is, both the Idea of the war machine (as a force beyond combating bodies) and becoming-woman as a relation to personification and sense that has abandoned identifiable and reliable content, do violence to good thinking. This is in two senses. First, there is a way in which this concept of becoming-woman has remained inassimilable in theory and has functioned to consolidate both a state of war, and a virile and paranoid mode of secrecy: either we need to make this concept work by restoring it to sense, or get to the heart of Deleuze's good sense beyond such messy notions. Second, becoming-woman opens a new mode of persona, where there is neither a feminist *use* of Deleuze nor a Deleuze that is allowed to develop within feminism while the masters get along with the work of Deleuze as a good and upright thinker and an object of Deleuze studies. If this concept enters the corpus of Deleuze and Guattari in an awkward and violent manner, it does so as a provocation and weapon that suggests – audaciously – that the one thing worse than a terrain of bickering, chatting, squabbling women with no real sense of the good is a perpetual philosophical peace in which problems are managed in reasonable conversations. Becoming-feminine considered through these two remarks regarding the war machine and the secret is at once a refusal of transcendence – some ultimate or final ground across which, or for which, combat takes place; at the same time it is a mode of relations without centre, ground, limiting polity, predefined stratification or object. But this does not preclude truth. On the contrary: truth is not some ground *given through* perspectives and styles, *for the truth is that there are styles.* 'Life' is not some One or secret that recedes and withdraws but is an infinite swarm of chaos, given and lived in moments of minimal order. If we were to read Deleuze and Guattari's becoming-woman according to the logic of internal pragmatics that it suggests then it would lead, I would suggest, to a different mode of writing: not a writing that either follows from a proper master, nor a writing that presents itself as the master. Such writing would be chatter: a multiplicity of voices that creates a pattern, a field of force, but does so without external justification. This would be different, also, from Deleuze's notion of 'taking a philosopher from behind,' which for all its irreverence still suggests a rebellion against the father. To think of a different mode of conceptual persona – the feminist conceptual persona – along the line suggested by becoming-woman and secrecy would enable a new mode of combat, a new voice or style that is no longer that of *the* philosopher who attaches to a concept, but something like a dissonance that distributes a field of phrases, response, questions and styles – never sure of *who* is speaking, and often – perhaps – rendering the secret master of the text indiscernible, imperceptible. If we consider women as a historically constituted group, not defined essentially, but produced as an identifiable social body through culture and history, then a philosopher who creates a concept of 'becoming-woman' and then goes on to see this mode of becoming as transitional certainly does appear to be appropriating or cannabilising feminism for the sake of a philosophical end. But if we consider woman as a new mode of creating problems where the production of questions opens a new terrain, and does not set itself in exclusive disjunction (Deleuze *or* Derrida, Badiou *or* Deleuze) then we move from theory as the creation of territories to theory as the positive production of nomadic thought.

As concluding example, I would cite Elizabeth Grosz's *Chaos, Territory, Art* (2008), for it is marked by three features, at least, that indicate a new mode of persona. First, this book does not take a philosopher (or philosophy, or theory) 'from behind.' It leaves its philosopher behind. It is as though Grosz has decided not to care about Deleuze's ontology, about his war with Kant, Hegel or Derrida; instead the lectures ask how we might look at art if we think of art not as an object (delimitable, with definitions) but as something that would make us perceive birdsong, fish, stones and bodies differently. Second, it takes contemporary Australian indigenous art, not as what art truly or properly is, but as something that has occurred, here and now, and that has left behind the tortured post-colonial annihilations of whether 'we' can encounter the 'other.' It simply looks at these artworks – not as the body of an Other who might give the lost secret of the West – but as they are presented, displayed, as creating a space. Finally, and subsequently, it is this absence of reverent scholarship to Deleuze as master thinker, and to ethics as some approach to a radical other who might restore one's status as a subject, that marks out a new persona. For this is not a book at war with others; there is no marking out of one's own terrain as the next step in a development of hypotheses, or as a break with the blindness of a past condemned to distance from the great secret.

So we might at one and the same time affirm the necessity of thinking of the feminist philosopher as conceptual persona: it is she who asks *whose* discourse, whose statement, whose subjection, performance, passion or negativity is expressed in this or that specific dissonance. At the same time, as *feminist*, this persona is not a figure defined by its active predicates – the one who doubts, affirms, negates and arrives at certainty – but is in a pattern of dissonance. Thus we could consider Rosi Braidotti's feminist subject (in *Patterns of Dissonance*) and Grosz's performance of an enquiry into art without asking 'what is art essentially?' in contrast with Deleuze's description of the Leibnizian monad, where each soul is composed of all the perceptions, affections, events and encounters that constitute its singular unfolding of infinity, (and with Deleuze's concomitant history of philosophical concepts and personae who act to reconfigure the entire plane with each of their textual creations). Leibniz's monad is harmonious: each soul sings its own tune, but because each soul is an expression of one infinite divine world, there is a resulting and felicitous harmony. Braidotti insists on dissonance, both because the tunes sung or expressed are not expressions of a preceding, implied, or divinely unfolded ground, and because no soul sings alone. Similarly, in Grosz there is a distance taken from Deleuze studies, and from philosophy *of* art, with there being less of a war on other thinkers, than a positive war or battle in composing strands of birdsong, buildings, human paintings, dance and sexuality (whatever that turns out to be). There is a din of voices: the dissonance presupposes that we can chart, think and trace the dissonances that make up any terrain, but the pattern of this dissonance has neither a transcendent origin, nor a pre-given goal of possible or ideal harmonisation. The din or dissonance is irreducible because voices cannot be uncoupled, nor can they step outside or above the cacophony. The subject is nomadic, in a constant state of metamorphosis and transposition, not just because it is one fragment of an open infinite that is never given, but because it is coupled; this persona is in dialogue or polylogue, at once different from any single system of matrix, and different *to* (or in relations of constantly differing difference) with the others with whom it is attached.

I therefore invite the reader of this volume to regard its opening onto chaos – its clear absence of a grasp of Deleuze – as the beginning of a problem, as an open secret.

References

Badiou, Alain (1999) *Manifesto for Philosophy*, trans. Norman Madarasz, Albany, NY: State University of New York Press.

Badiou, Alain (2005) *Being and Eveny*, trans. Oliver Feltham. London: Continuum.

Bergson, Henri (1911) *Laughter; An Essay on the Meaning of the Comic*. New York: Macmillan.

Bergson, Henri (1935) *The Two Sources of Morality and Religion*, trans. R. Ashley Audra and Cloudesley Brereton, with the assistance of W. Horsfall Carter, New York: H. Holt.

Braidotti, Rosi (1991) *Patterns of Dissonance: A Study of Women in Contemporary Philosophy*, trans. Elizabeth Guild, New York: Routledge.

Damasio, Antonio R. (1994) *Descartes' Error: Emotion, Reason, and the Human Brain*, New York: Putnam.

Damasio, Antonio R. (2003) *Looking for Spinoza: Joy, Sorrow, and the Feeling Brain*, Orlando: Harcourt.

De Landa, Manuel (2006) *A New Philosophy of Society: Assemblage Theory and Social Complexity*, London: Continuum.

Deleuze, Gilles and Claire Parnet (1987) *Dialogues*, trans. Hugh Tomlinson and Barbara Habberjam, London: Athlone Press.

Deleuze, Gilles (1990) *The Logic of Sense*, trans. Mark Lester with Charles Stivale, ed. Constantin V. Boundas, New York: Columbia University Press.

Deleuze, Gilles (1993) *The Fold: Leibniz and the Baroque*, trans. Tom Conley, Minneapolis: University of Minnesota Press.

Deleuze, Gilles (1994) *Difference and Repetition*, trans. Paul Patton, London: Athlone.

Deleuze, Gilles (2006) *Nietzsche and Philosophy*, trans. Hugh Tomlinson, New York: Columbia University Press.

Flanagan, Owen J. (2007) *The Really Hard Problem: Meaning in a Material World*, Cambridge, MA: MIT Press.

Grosz, E. A. (2008) *Chaos, Territory, Art: Deleuze and the Framing of the Earth*, New York: Columbia University Press.

Habermas, Jurgen (1992) *Postmetaphysical Thinking: Philosophical Essays*, trans. William Mark Hohengarten, Cambridge, MA: MIT Press.

Hallward, Peter (2006) *Out of this World: Deleuze and the Philosophy of Creation*, London: Verso.

Hansen, Mark (2000) 'Becoming Other as Creative Involution?: Contextualizing Deleuze and Guattari's Biophilosophy', *Postmodern Culture* 11.1 (September).

Irigaray, Luce (1996) *I Love to You: Sketch for a Felicity within History*, trans. Alison Martin, New York: Routledge.

Jardine, Alice (1985) *Gynesis: Configurations of Woman and Modernity*, Ithaca: Cornell University Press.

Lambert, Gregg (2006) *Who's Afraid of Deleuze and Guattari?*, London: Continuum.

Maturana, Humberto and Francisco J. Varela (1987) *The Tree of Knowledge: The Biological Roots of Human Understanding*, 1st edn, Boston: New Science Library.

Rorty, Richard (1998) *Truth and Progress*, Cambridge: Cambridge University Press.

Thompson, Evan (2007) *Mind in Life: Biology, Phenomenology, and the Sciences of Mind*, Cambridge, MA: Belknap Press of Harvard University Press.

Varela, Francisco J., Evan Thompson, Eleanor Rosch (1991) *The Embodied Mind: Cognitive Science and Human Experience*, Cambridge, MA: MIT Press.

Zizek, Slavoj (1999) *The Ticklish Subject: The Absent Centre of Political Ontology*, London: Verso.

Notes

1. I use the term awkwardness here as suggested by Bergson's (1911) essay on laughter. It is when the human sensory-motor organism does not function efficiently – as in slap-stick or 'screwball' comedy where actions and conversations occur in a manner that displays the body's rigidity – that we are given a sense of just how organized the human animal has become, and therefore how it might be otherwise.

DOI: 10.3366/E1750224108000330

Introduction Part II

Jami Weinstein

In her editorial introduction to this volume, Colebrook mischievously and provocatively chooses to leave the reader with 'the beginning of a problem, an open secret.' Before doing so, she meticulously outlines one of the central issues feminists have had with deploying the work of Deleuze and Guattari: how are we to understand that pesky *becoming-woman* formulation? As she rightly describes it, feminists often believe that the task of 'grasping Deleuze' hinges on whether the concept of becoming-woman is 'good or bad feminism,' wondering how to make sense of two male philosophers granting women 'not only a role in thinking, but in life as such.' As Colebrook ultimately points out, these are the wrong questions to ask, the wrong concerns to have. Taking becoming-woman in this direction means looking at this concept as a momentary lapse in philosophical rigor, as somehow separate and apart from analysis of the creative and transformative ontological issues Deleuze exposes – those that are the domain of real (read: male) philosophers. This, as she claims, has 'disastrous and embarrassing' consequences – one could almost say it is evidence for a self-marginalizing process produced by feminists who want to perpetuate the need for feminism, more on this later. Since the project of grasping Deleuze's work itself is false according to an understanding of his work, we need to pay heed to Colebrook's reformulation of the so-called 'becoming-woman problem' as a tool for creating dissonance via refigured relationships to the war machine and its concomitant secret. We could thus allow it to spawn new lines of ontological flight, rather than closing down thinking, and we could understand it not as a lapse but as a central element of the rigorous ontological reclamation project that typifies the work of Deleuze.

What Colebrook's introduction suggests is that a productive linkage between Deleuze and feminism can only be made on the back of a more wide-spread dispelling of pesky concepts and theoretical and conceptual misdirection, even if this means opening into the chaos and ceding hard-fought wars that at least seemed to create new possibilities of more libratory foundational ground. The force and creativity of

Deleuzian ontology can indeed be harnessed for feminist purposes but to do this we may need to bite the bullet on a variety of unproductive interpretations of the war machine. To this end, I propose we dredge up one other pesky concept: that of the fundamental ontology of sexual difference. If we are to 'bring the secret' through becoming-woman as Deleuze suggests (Deleuze and Guattari, 1987: 287), and part of exposing the secret is to open ourselves up to chaos and dissonance as Colebrook suggests, we also need to attend to the question of sexual difference anew, with a Deleuzian flair for truly transformative materialist ontology, rather that get fixated on any particular assemblage that gives the appearance of being foundational, even if that seems libratory.

In *Deleuze and Feminist Theory* Colebrook asked the question: 'Is Sexual Difference a Problem?' On the tenth anniversary of that publication, and in light of her own hints in the introductory essay to this volume that this problem *is* a problem, at least in the Deleuzian sense, I would like to now revisit her question. Yet, rather than repeating her question, I will take her suggestion that it is a problem and attempt to answer her two-fold call: (1) to redirect feminist interpretation on at least this pesky concept and (2) to think differently through the question of sexual difference. I will do this through a repetition of difference, asking not 'is sexual difference a problem?' but rather, if sexual difference is taken as a real problem, the sort that evades embarrassing and divisively marginalizing consequences for feminist theory, how might it be, as a concept, 'inventive: creating new concepts, new questions and new problems.' (Colebrook, 2000: 114) I do not pretend I will give an exhaustive account of the new concepts, questions, and problems that the problem of sexual difference creates. I wish only to investigate and provoke thinking on one fertile ground: zoontology and the repudiation of Enlightenment Humanism.

Sexual difference as a concept has been fantastically successful in helping us realize that we are living under an oppressive ontology of the One, a logic that pervades all aspects of thought, science, language, culture, psychoanalysis, philosophy, etc. But what it helps us *think through* via its prescient claim to move toward an (at least) dual ontology is the possibility of an ontology based on a fluid multiplicity. I see in the logic of sexual difference theory the possibility of re-imagining human ontology and repudiating Enlightenment Humanism, not simply by redefining human ontology as the ontology of two irreconcilable subjects but by using the concept of sexual difference to catapult ontology beyond humanism more generally through taking account of animality. As Colebrook noted, '(i)f sexual difference is not theorised *from* a metaphysics, but is confronted as a problem, then we might take the issues of sexual difference and use them to *think*.' (Colebrook, 2000: 126) Thus, rather than conceptualize sexual difference as the constitutive foundation for all differences, or theorize sexual difference as a fundamental ontology, I would like to use sexual difference as a starting point for thinking differently about human ontology more generally. I believe this move toward fluid multiplicity is part of the sexual difference line of flight, virtually present within the concept itself. It is taking the concept of sexual difference in this direction that it becomes a proper philosophical and ontological project rather than merely a crumb on which feminist philosophers can chew.

Deleuze himself recognizes that there is no end only a beginning of a new question in the realization of sexual difference when he remarks about women's 'true ontological status:'

> the being of woman is never realized, and can never be realized without contradiction, without dissolution... Woman is neither object nor subject... she is not yet that which is; she is the *élan* of the object towards subjectivity. Neither an object in the world nor the subject of a possible world. She is not a subject, she does not reach being. (Deleuze, 2002: 23)

In other words, the realization of sexual difference, women's subjectivity, would only serve to dissolve sexual difference itself. This is the bullet we must bite in order to more productively engage Deleuze for feminist purposes: that subjectivity, once reached, is its own dissolution. But to what end?

If my suggestion that the concept of sexual difference has virtually within it a more fundamental question of an ontology of fluid multiplicity is accurate, that would be the reason we should be willing to bite that bullet. In what follows, I will sketch this trajectory and why I think pursuing this line of flight might be even more productive in the long run for feminists.

PHILOSOPHICAL CONCEPTS

If we are to take feminist philosophy seriously *qua* philosophy, and we grant Deleuze and Guattari's claim that, '(p)hilosophy is the discipline that involves *creating* concepts,' (Deleuze and Guattari, 1994: 5) then we must acknowledge sexual difference as a concept. As Deleuze and Guattari note, however, 'concepts need conceptual personae that play a part in their definition.' (Deleuze and Guattari, 1994: 2) Given that concepts are multiplicities, at least double or triple, (Deleuze and Guattari, 1994: 15) investigating the concept of sexual difference must reveal conceptual personae aside from feminist philosophers who play a part in their definition. Before revealing the outcome of this analysis, we need to think through this theory of the concept a bit more.

Deleuze and Guattari argue that, 'All concepts are connected to problems without which they would have no meaning and which can themselves only be isolated or understood as their solution emerges.' (Deleuze and Guattari, 1994: 16) As Elizabeth Grosz explains, 'every concept requires a delimitation to give it some 'identity,' however historically provisional; it also requires a ground, a mode of connection to the world.' (Grosz, 2005: 159) She continues that, 'They are connected to the resolution of problems or questions, for it is problems or questions which occasion concepts, and concepts are developed as a mode of addressing questions.' (Grosz, 2005: 159) What I will argue here is that the concept of sexual difference is historically provisional even though it emerges from a material connection to the world. Our need for it is connected to the resolution of a problem, the problem of correcting sexism for example. Once we have understood the problem and the concept, as we will observe, we realize that the concept is not about ontological differences between men and women at all, but a logic. It is this logic that pushes the philosophical value to a deeper level.

Deleuze and Guattari tell us that, '(t)he concept speaks the event, not the essence or the thing.' (Deleuze and Guattari, 1994: 21) This is in line with sexual difference as a concept as long as we recognize, as Irigaray certainly does in acknowledging it as not yet realized, that the concept is, 'the contour, the configuration, the constellation of an event to come.' (Deleuze and Guattari, 1994: 32–3) However, Irigaray and others argue that the event to come is the materialization of a fundamental ontology of sexual difference, the coming into existence of the subject woman. I think that this is *part* of the event to come, but stopping there does not tell the full story of the more important event that the concept of sexual difference can bring. Proposing sexual difference as foundational simply sets up new questions. Thus, if sexual difference is a concept, as I am arguing it is, it is more properly a 'center of vibrations' (Deleuze and Guattari, 1994: 23) or a dissonance (as Colebrook, in her introduction, suggests becoming-woman to be) than it is about some ontological truth of the matter. As is the case with all concepts, according to Deleuze and Guattari, if a concept is unable to constitute itself, it is likely the result of it being mired in other problems. Further, perhaps due to the vibrations and forces within the concept itself, it evokes an event that helps create future concepts to better resolve the problems to which it was originally linked. To wit, I am suggesting that the inability of sexual difference to materialize is linked to the problem of humanism in general.

THE LOGIC OF SEXUAL DIFFERENCE

In the domain of contemporary feminist ontology, the trend seems to be to argue (following the work of Luce Irigaray) that because *le féminin* has been unspoken, unwritten, and non-existent in the hegemonic versions of human ontology, we need to attend first to the business of speaking and writing it into existence. What both generates and follows from this project is the claim that there has been a grave error deep within the backbone of our mainstream understanding of human ontology. That is to say that ontology up until now has been seen as monadic, fundamentally singular, about the One — where the phallocentrically patriarchal model codes all knowledge, language, science, forms of representation, the symbolic order, and socioeconomic structures as masculine, woman is relegated to the untheorized lack. What sexual difference theory has brought to the fore is that human ontology is, rather than the masculine One and the feminine lack, an ontology of (at least) Two—where woman and man are irreducible others.

I am sympathetic to this project, for it is true that the concept of woman has not been historically a concept of woman at all but rather 'not-man.' In the ontology of the One the human becomes man and not-man, woman never even enters the picture. Woman has been (un)conceptualized into a void, or pure negation of the masculine, but has never been theorized as a positive subject. I do not argue with this analysis. There is something intuitively and even logically true about this story. However, what I want to argue is that this story, while accurate, is not the story of a *fundamental* ontology, the precondition for all other differences. As a fundamental ontology, sexual difference would be considered 'the difference that precedes the entities it produces' (Grosz, 2005: 174), not merely a social difference attributed to bodies of particular kinds. I want to claim that achieving a world in which we have a well articulated, irreducible, dual sexual ontology would not exhaust the human ontological picture. Rather, it is merely a first stage along the path to understanding what it is to *be* human. In other words, sexual difference ontology does tell part of the story of becoming human, the part that delimits what it is to be human. If our interest is what it is to *become* human, we cannot dub that story the most fundamental of stories of human ontology. Thus, we must have neglected to interrogate a deeper question virtually present within the concept of sexual difference.

UNDOING SEXUAL DIFFERENCE (IMPERCEPTIBILITY)

So, what I propose is that once we arrive at the point where we can understand sexual difference as a concept and understand the logic of the One it exposes, we then need to think through it and propel it further philosophically. By that I mean that we need to undo sexual difference once we finally conceived it, in order not to remain egotistically anthropocentric. But this undoing is not a return to the state we are now in, where women are lack or merely 'difference from a norm,' it is not a return to the humanism of the past with its hidden and untheorized phallocentrism. It is a repetition of difference, pure difference, not a repetition of the same.

I know this logic will worry those feminists who would be loathe to relinquish the hard won subjectivity we were (and still are) denied for fear of a return to the patriarchal sameness, solidity, false binaries, and domination of the ontology of the One. But their fears are unwarranted. As I said, this is not a return to the same. It should be noted that these same feminists would also be hesitant about, if not completely antagonistic to, the idea that a fully successful feminist strategy is to aim for its own eradication — in other words, once the goals of the movement are achieved, we will have reached a state in which there is no longer a need for feminism. The misunderstanding of the goal of feminism (as recognition and visibility rather than imperceptibility) is one of the reasons I think that the problem of sexual difference is a false problem: most advocates of sexual difference as a fundamental ontology would theorize sexual difference into perpetuity and thus establish a basis upon which feminism would always exist. For example, according to Irigaray, sexual difference of an ontologically fundamental kind has not yet happened. Thus, it remains a virtual possibility, one that may never fully be realized and one for which we cannot have a blueprint. According to Grosz, this means that the time of sexual difference is the future. However, if the time of sexual difference is always already the future, feminism must take as its ultimate goal simply the perpetuation of an unrealized virtual force.

On the contrary, I am inclined to argue following Deleuze and Guattari that the ultimate goal of human becoming is becoming imperceptible. This means, following Grosz, that 'the future feminine must render itself obsolete or the object of profound and even inhuman (or imperceptible) becomings rather than itself rest on the forms of femininity as they have been represented and idealized in sexual indifference, or within patriarchy as it has existed up to now.'

(Grosz, 2005: 177) This is, as Grosz says, 'a politics of imperceptibility and acts not one of identities and recognition.' (Grosz, 2005: 189) Becoming-woman and its underlying sexual difference would be useless concepts if measured according to visibility and identity. They would serve only as tidbits to distract feminist philosophers from the real work of philosophy. Feminist strategies would be better aimed toward mobilizing these concepts toward a politics of imperceptibility, as Deleuze and Guattari themselves recognize when they assemble the triad: becoming-woman, becoming-animal, becoming-imperceptible. This feminist move toward the imperceptible, suggested by Grosz, would take the following form:

> Instead of a politics of recognition, in which subjected groups and minorities strive for a validated and affirmed place in public life, feminist politics should, I believe, now consider the affirmation of a politics of imperceptibility, leaving its traces and effects everywhere but never being able to be identified with a person, group, or organization. It is not a politics of visibility, of recognition and of self-validation, but a process of self-marking that constitutes oneself in the very model of that which oppresses and opposes the subject. The imperceptible is that which the inhuman musters... (Grosz, 2005: 194)

We find the key in her last sentence, also found in her argument on page 177 cited above: becoming-woman and sexual difference *qua* concepts tend toward *in*humanity, a deterritorialization of the human, a repudiation of humanism, a transhuman perspective. It is here we find the move to a transspecies zoontology virtually present in the concept of sexual difference; it is here that the open secret is revealed and the deeper philosophical problem can begin.

MOBILIZING THE LOGIC OF THE ONE—THE MOVE TO ZOONTOLOGY

The recent attention given by feminist theorists to the value of questions of animality and the concomitant desire to refigure the relation between humans and animals reveals the need for a more subtle and profound zoontological theory. Once we do have a working zoontological theory, however, we must determine its place in relation to human ontology; it is important to come to terms with how this shift in focus toward the zoontological might fit with other theories of decidedly central importance to these theorists. Notably here, the issue of an ontology of sexual difference. We need to reassess the value of maintaining sexual difference as the fundamental ontology in light of a move away from humanism in general, for sexual difference seems predicated on at least some form of humanism, or at least an historical speciesism.[1] Though the positioning of sexual difference as a fundamental ontology is undeniably controversial, even among feminist philosophers, we need to conceptualize how or if that view might gel with a fundamental transhumanism based on zoontological premises. We must also understand how marshalling the logic of the One invented through the concept of sexual difference for the task of deconstructing humanism's inherent speciesism actualizes the virtual concept present in sexual difference theory in such a way that a more productive relationship between becoming-woman and the war machine can be discerned and the conceptual persona of the Feminist Philosopher becomes a proper philosopher.

To recapitulate, following sexual difference theorists like Irigaray, the goal of feminism should be to move from the logic of sexual indifference, or the logic of the One, to the logic of (at least) Two through the articulation of woman and, thus, an ontological sexual difference. Irigaray holds this ontology as the most fundamental human ontology. I agree that this is an important phase in the deconstruction of one insidious hierarchy embedded in Enlightenment Humanism. However, we must not stop there, it is merely an initial step. If we stop here, we once again arrive at a logic of the One: the humanistic, speciesist logic of the One. For, what it is to be animal in the post-enlightenment world is to be untheorized lack, or not-human. In other words, once the logic of the One is detected as virtual within the concept of sexual difference, we need to harness it to think through another important ontological piece of the humanism puzzle: the logic of the One present in the human/non-human animal binary.[2] What needs to take place then, is the move to what I would call a transspecies zoontology[3]. In moving to this element of the deconstruction of Enlightenment Humanism, we must take heed of the advice to become-imperceptible. This involves biting the bullet and undoing the human sexual difference now conceptually articulated. In other words, to fully realize imperceptibility, we must transform the (albeit hard won, if it has even been won at all) logic of the Two with a logic of fluid multiplicity and this means that the irreducible man-woman binary will multiply both internally and externally. It is here that we arrive at a *more* fundamental conception of human ontology[4] and we can grasp the philosophical importance the concept of sexual difference has virtually within it.

What I suggest is that we expand and multiply the logic of the (at least) Two to the logic of the imperceptible multiple in order to deterritorialize the human and *become*, paradoxically more fully human. In the dichotomy of human and non-human animal, we establish another mythology of an ontological dualism that does not really exist: a human/non-human animal *in*difference. Underlying this is the presupposition that there is one thing human and one thing animal to which we are referring. If we acknowledge (via sexual difference theory) that there are at least two irreducible ontological human entities (woman and man), we must then admit that counterposing some singular concept of the human against some singular concept animal is misguided. This demonstrates a key misinterpretation of the speciesist logic of the One without even attending to the fact that a singular notion of 'the animal' is simply specious. Thus, if we counterpose a multiplicity human against a multiplicity animal, we reduce our analysis to mere nonsense if it is founded on singular logics. For what is a human? Against which animal is it measured?

In recognizing the fluid multiple ontology called forth through these dual logics of the One, we must note that this is part of the function of all becomings, as Deleuze and Guattari remark that, 'becoming and multiplicity are the same thing. [I]ts variations and dimensions are immanent to it.' (Deleuze and Guattari 1987: 249) Becoming is also figured in contrast to teleology, a sentiment subtly echoed in sexual difference theory. To wit, Deleuze and Guattari claim that, 'a line of becoming is not defined by points that it connects, or by points that compose it; on the contrary, it passes between points, it comes up through the middle... a line of becoming has neither beginning nor end, departure nor arrival, origin nor destination... a line of becoming has only a middle.' (Deleuze and Guattari 1987: 293) Irigaray, too, recognizes this when she advises, '(b)e what you are becoming, without clinging to what might have been, what you might yet be.' (Irigaray, 1985: 214) The point of this process of becoming is not to transform into another pure entity or being but rather to become other and ultimately become imperceptible.

This move toward a fundamental transspecies zoontology is located within the realm of a Deleuzian pure difference (or what I would call horizontal difference) rather than a 'difference from a norm' (or what I would call a vertical difference). It is a return to a concept of human ontology that is not founded on sexual *in*difference (this state is one in which sexual difference has *never* passed through a stage in which the concept of sexual difference has already been articulated, much less been considered fundamental) but rather one that is *no longer* founded on sexual difference; it is an extrapolation out from the ontological Two into the plane of the multiple. In other words, it is a return of sorts but not a going back to the same. It is an ontology of fluid multiplicity with sexual difference as *no longer* fundamental predicated on a prior moment of sexual difference as conceptually fundamental.

In conclusion, for the larger project of deconstructing Enlightenment Humanism, demarcating sexual difference does seem like an important place to start, since it is from within that concept that we find the logic of the One, a central tool for unpacking the human/non-human animal binary. Additionally, from within the concept of sexual difference, we come to understand some of what has been left out of the *human* picture – woman. However, to call this ontology of sexual difference fundamental, the constitutive difference of all other differences, belies a deep-seated anthropocentrism. If we do not attend to the fact that claiming this as a fundamental ontology is a teleological error, we will be left in a revised form of humanism; it cannot be the ontology that precedes all other differences unless the so-called later stages of evolution are the only ones that count. Hence, what I have sketched here (albeit very schematically) is that, while sexual difference might be an interesting and even important difference, one for which we need to account, it is not the unique, most interesting, or fundamental difference typifying human being. However, the concept of sexual difference remains squarely philosophical and Feminist Philosophers become philosophers insofar as the concept they spawned contains all the virtual fodder necessary to do 'real' ontology. The concept of sexual difference contains the vibrations and the virtual logic that push us through the problem of humanism more fully. Thus, it is by thinking through the concept of sexual difference that we may be able to arrive at zoontology, a robustly *human* transspecies transhumanism.

DELEUZE AND FEMINIST PHILOSOPHY – THIS ISSUE

A quick gloss of the pieces in this volume shows that contemporary feminists working with Deleuze have come to terms with what Colebrook and I are both suggesting – that in order to produce a more productive linkage between Deleuze's work and the aims of feminist philosophy, we must do away with the pesky concepts, the philosophical crumbs, and *do* philosophy. We must think through becoming-woman and sexual difference to the more inventive philosophical concepts they produce. We must go beyond the good or evil, the marginalizing he said-she said approach, and attend to the creative ontological task that philosophical concepts present to us.

Colebrook suggests in *Deleuze and Feminist Theory* that:

(s)exual difference might open the question of different bodily compartments, different responses to the given within the given ... it might be time to think of the body in its various distributions. This would not mean offering a Deleuzian theory of the body, but would look at the body to think differently... Mightn't the anorexic body, which posits a radical disjunction between body-image, lived body and empirical body, disrupt the dreamed-of unity of the phenomenological subject?' (Colebrook, 2000: 125)

Branca Arsic, in her analysis of anorexia in this issue, answers Colebrook's call for that 'bodily philosophy' arguing that, '(a)norexia is both the process of experimenting with the form of the body – its resexualization – and the politics of disturbing the socially imposed order of everyday life.' Further, she does this without falling into the trap of doing a philosophy *of* the body. She understands this when she argues that, '(a)norexia should be understood to represent a particular strategy of resistance, and rescuing it from the inane ideology of an 'eating disorder,' as well as from the brunt theory of a 'consumption' neurosis is a function of such a resistance,' envisioning anorexia as an experimentation in line with Deleuze's Humean empiricism. Concluding that, '(i)f the main goal of the micropolitics of... anorexia is to invent the body of waves, the body without organs, then the success of such an experiment means, paradoxically, that the body without organs will never be fully realized, for such a realization is pure and simple death,' Arsic understands that feminist philosophers must meet the challenge of conceptual lack of origin and telos; they must see to it that we do not end up with the static, 'frozen body' potentially theorized by misdirected interpretations of becoming-woman and some reductive forms of the ontology of sexual difference.

Gillian Howie highlights the ways in which the micropolitics of becoming-woman are neither 'innocent nor without context.' Along the way through her careful philosophical argument about empircism and the relationship and slippages between ontology and epistemology, she reveals the material, corporal, ontological, and non-utopian means by which feminists can analyze this concept. While she agrees with its success at avoiding the 'dimorphic essentialism' implied in some versions of sexual difference, she cautions that we risk, 'de-contextualizing and appropriating the affective body.' She, argues that becoming-woman is a '*dis*embodiment... arguably at odds with any productive and beneficial social critique of invested desire... certainly a long way from feminist phenomenology.' In other words, citing Braidotti, she holds that, '(becoming-woman) is a theory of difference with no room for sexual difference.' According to what Colebrook and I have argued, and what Howie seems to be implying here, this may not necessarily be a conclusive failing of becoming-woman as a concept. Like Colebrook,

Howie seeks to rescue this concept from its theoretical uselessness by understanding the ways in which it, 'manages to reintroduce sexual difference, silently, through the back door.' She, thus, seems to call forth my argument (with a healthy bit of caution about how we might fall into the traps Colebrook outlined) about ways we might refigure our understanding of sexual difference. In other words, she demonstrates how becoming-woman speaks and thinks the open secret of the concept of sexual difference, configured not as an end but as a means.

Similarly, Tasmin Lorraine argues in this issue that:

> This division of humanity into two sexually differentiated groups obscures a wide range of social investments of the contemporary social field stratified into various configurations of power by highlighting sexed identity as key to determining who one is and how to live one's life. A variegated range of differences among human subjects is thus reduced in significance when compared to identification with one of the two categories, woman or man.

This clearly indicates that, while, as she states, 'sexed, gendered, and sexual identity are central features of the oedipal subject, making the question of sexual difference a crucial one,' as I have argued, its ultimate import may not be about a fundamental sexual difference at all. That, as she says, '(f)eminism, as a theoretical and pragmatic process, can intuit ways of living our sex and gender that are more affirming of the continuous range of variation in being sexed and gendered becoming-human entails.' In other words, that becoming-human through deterritorializing the human, or eradicating *humanism*, might be accomplished *through* sexual difference without sexual difference being assessed as teleologically fundamental. It might simply be the concept that provides the anti-humanist tools we need.

Rebecca Hill also subtly argues this point. In exposing Bergson's open system as implicitly sexed and phallocentric in its formulation of the relationship between life and matter, she claims that, 'Bergson's commitment to dualism can be read as symptomatic of a disavowal of a sexed hierarchy at the very heart of his open system.' She notes that '(t)he sexed hierarchy ... is perhaps most pronounced in his account of evolution,' which demonstrates, 'the valorisation of a hyper-masculine theory of life and corresponding devaluation of matter as feminine.' She hints at my argument that sexual difference can help us rethink Enlightenment Humanism when she implies that Bergson's sexed hierarchy of life over matter can be read as part of a more insidious humanist hierarchy. This can be seen where she claims that, '(f)or Bergson, Man is distinguished from animals by a difference in nature and presented as the 'end' of evolution. He warns that Man is the 'end' in a special sense . . . because he alone allowed life to triumph over the 'obstacle' matter.' The suggestion here seems to be that thinking through sexed differences and hierarchies pushes us right back to questions of humanism in general and to the important ontological war traditionally waged between human and non-human animals or, as Hill calls it, the 'phallic anthropomorphism.'

Dorothea Olkowski, in a creative exploration of logic and the feminine, also touches on themes of embodiment and animality; these motifs, like the feminine, are traditionally associated with the underground world inhabited by Alice when she descends into Wonderland. Olkowski argues that, 'Wonderland may not be all that wonderful,' if indeed the formal structures upholding traditional logic are abandoned. In the end, Olkowski concludes that there is a hidden sex difference at the heart of becoming-woman because, 'woman has to become-woman for man to become-woman,' which 'evinces a fundamental binarism at the heart of (Deleuze and Guattari's) philosophy.' If her final assertion is correct, however, that because Alice 'understands the limits of language and logic, the limitless world of possibilities, a world without causality and identity, without the arrow of times, without signification or reference,' she is, 'a thinker . . . a philosopher,' we are once again back at the question of what the concepts becoming-woman and sexual difference *do* philosophically. And we have returned to the question of concepts. Her references to embodiment and animality, I think, once again provide the clue. For, a world (Wonderland) without identity and causality ensconced in a world of traditional logic *is* Irigaray's phallocentric world of the not yet existing *féminin* subject. On this read of becoming-woman, feminist philosophers are unable to *do* philosophy and remain trapped chewing philosophical crumbs alongside the man's world of *real* ontology. But, Olkowski's various references to animality and corporality lurking beneath the surface questions of the logic of the One and the identities it both produces and erases beckon us to the *philosophical* concepts virtually present in becoming-woman and an ontology of sexual difference. These questions also ask feminists to do philosophy, ontology, and ultimately repudiate humanism at a more fundamental level.

So it is clear that this volume brings together a variety of feminist linkages to Deleuze that return feminist philosophy to the job of philosophy. We hope this will serve as an inspiration to other philosophers who seek to continue to unpack the open secrets.

References

Colebrook, Claire. (2000) "Is Sexual Difference a Problem?" in Buchanan, Ian, and Claire Colebrook, eds., *Deleuze and Feminist Theory*, Edinburgh: Edinburgh University Press.

Deleuze, Gilles. (2002) "Description of Woman: For a Philosophy of the Sexed Other." Trans. Keith Faulkner, *Angelaki: Journal of Theoretical Humanities*, Vol. 7, No. 3, December 2002.

Deleuze, Gilles and Claire Parnet. (1987) *Dialogues*, Trans. Hugh Tomlinson and Barbara Habberjam, London: Athlone Press.

Deleuze, Gilles and Guattari, Félix: (1987) *A Thousand Plateaus: Capitalism and Schizophrenia*, Trans. Brian Massumi, Minneapolis: University of Minnesota Press.

——: (1994) *What is Philosophy?*, Trans. Hugh Tomlinson and Graham Burchell, New York: Columbia University Press.

Grosz, Elizabeth. (2005) *Time Travels: Feminism, Nature, Power*, Crow's Nest, Australia: Allen and Unwin.

Irigaray, Luce. (1985) *This Sex Which Is Not One*, Trans. Catherine Porter, Ithaca, N.Y.: Cornell University Press.

Notes

1. While I acknowledge that many non-human animals reproduce sexually, this is certainly not the case for all living non-human creatures. It is important here to recognize the multiplicity always part of the construct 'animal' for, neglecting to do so already begs the question of the humanistic logic of the One, where 'the non-human animal' is a singular lack to the singular human One.
2. I must acknowledge that the same argument could possibly be made in reverse. That is to say, if we started with the human/non-human animal distinction, detected its logic of the One, we would still be left with the problem of sexual difference, especially since the case could easily be made that many animals reproduce sexually. So what I am suggesting here is that the ontology of sexual difference is a necessary part of the deconstruction of Enlightenment Humanism but so is zoontology. However, my suspicion is that zoontology would trump the ontology of sexual difference along the path toward foundational ontologies insofar as it gets to the core of the humanist logic and its human chauvinism.
3. I will not take the liberty of presenting my theory of transspecies zoontology here nor will I explain why it more thoroughly responds to core problems of Enlightenment Humanism. However, suffice it to say (as I have said elsewhere) that the concept 'human' has been a relatively modern construction, one that relies on a clear distinction from what is deemed to be 'animal.' It is precisely the moment that 'animal' came to be seen as other to man that Foucault, in the *Order of Things* indicates when he asserts that man as an epistemological entity, as a species, came into being. Humanity then became the subject in contrast to the animal object. But, as Nietzsche forewarned, this was the great error of the arrogant modern man.
4. I am not proposing that there is a single fundamental ontology or ever could be, as I am not sure that trying to determine a foundation can ever be a productive strategy for progressive political battles.

DOI: 10.3366/E1750224108000342

The Experimental Ordinary: Deleuze on Eating and Anorexic Elegance

Branka Arsic   State University of New York, Albany

Abstract

The paper discusses Deleuze's concept of the feminine through exploration of the questions of eating, cooking, and specifically anorexia, as well as an 'anorexic relation' to fashion and dressing. It argues that anorexia should be understood as a micro-political experimentation in fashioning one's own body on its flight to becoming woman. In accordance with Deleuze's ontology of the surface, the anorexic body can be seen as the invention of the BWO that forms an assemblage with clothes and, in so becoming different, invents for itself different desires.

Keywords: body, ascesis, anorexia, eating, cooking, fashion, desire.

Feminine desires activate various processes in Deleuze. They set intensities on paths called 'becoming-woman'; they gesture towards secrets; or else they make pacts with larval selves so as to change more global gendered or mental set ups. They also activate a series of micro-political practices of asceticism, which destabilise the mind to the point of doing away with persons. Masochism is one such pragmatics: in experimenting with pain it works to unsettle the formation of personal boundaries. However, the varieties of ascetic politics – masochism, anorexia, drug addiction, alcoholism – differ, even if sharing some features. They are all 'assembled' by a desire that experiments on and with borders and they are all seduced by anomalous or abominable unions, while producing different effects: 'If the machine is not a mechanism, and if the body is not an organism, it is always then that desire assembles. But it is not in the same way as a masochist assembles, or a drug addict, or an alcoholic, or an anorexic. Etc.' (Deleuze 1987: 109). Whereas masochism works with waves and rhythms, hence often outside the specular, anorexia works within the domain of visual perception. It represents experimentation with the production of visual signs, disturbing the way we distinguish among forms of organs or bodies, persons or sexes. Whereas masochism is a micro-politics that operates between the 'I' and the 'You' in order to negate the force of identity politics and explore ways in which I becomes You, anorexia operates between the 'I' and smaller social groups, such as, for instance, a family. Whereas masochism is about restructuring the organs of one's own body, anorexia restructures the relations among many bodies and signs: food, clothes, drinks, sexuality. Anorexia is thus both the process of experimenting with the form of the body – its resexualisation – and the politics of disturbing the socially imposed order of everyday life. In what follows I will examine how codes that dominate female bodies are turned against themselves in anorexia and employed in the contrivance of new experimental femininities.

Deleuze's understanding of anorexia differs fundamentally from the common understanding of *anorexia nervosa*. To label it 'nervosa' is itself ideologically charged and so signals its own political position. To call anorexia a neurosis is to suggest the answer to its enigma. Hence, according to the famous reading offered by Freud and Breuer, hysterical nervousness is the repetition of reminiscence; the anorexic suffers from an unsuccessfully repressed past trauma. Anorexia would thus have its origin in a type of genealogical disorder. Whereas most psychic disorders obey the dictum 'when the cause ceases the effect ceases,' in hysterical nervousness this genealogical principle is reversed and the cause finds a way to survive and directly affect the body:

> We may reverse the dictum 'cessante cause cessat efectus' ['when the cause ceases the effect ceases'] and conclude... that the determining process continues to operate in some way or other for years – not indirectly, through a chain of intermediate causal links, but as a directly releasing cause – just as a psychical pain that is remembered in waking consciousness still provokes a lachrymal secretion long after the event. Hysterics suffer mainly from reminiscences. (Breuer and Freud 1956: 58)

Healing anorexic nervousness would involve imposing a genealogical order by curing the 'origin;' it would require the analyst to detect the cause and then to try to weaken its force, so that once the cause ceased so would the effect. Such ideas of origin, order, genealogy and reminiscence guide this interpretation; and while it remains important in signaling the power of affection in anorexia – as a directly inflicted pain – it nevertheless hides the fact that the origin exists only as the phantasm of origin, hence itself a 'cause' of neurosis, thus blocking the access to the 'nature' of anorexia.

Anorexic Betrayals

To call anorexia an eating disorder is to suggest not only the existence of a phantasmatic origin but also a fantasised order, since it is to insist that there is a proper eating order. In contrast to that, Deleuze will argue that the idea of eating order confuses the fact that the organism has to live on something (but on what, precisely?) with a particular order of eating: 'The anorexic void has nothing to do with a lack, it is on the contrary a way of escaping the organic constraint of lack and hunger at the mechanical mealtime' (Deleuze 1987: 110). Finally, to say that the anorexic has a different image of her own body, which does not adequately represent the 'real' shape of it – to say for instance, that she sees her body as big in spite of the 'fact' that it is becoming thinner – is to suppose the normalising instance of a shared perception: one should see one's own body the way everybody else sees it.

In contrast to these readings of anorexia Deleuze will claim that the anorexic is not driven by a refusal of the body but rather by the refusal of a certain ideology of the body. The anorexic refuses the idea of the 'organised,' or organic body: 'It is not a matter of a refusal of the body, it is a matter of a refusal of the organism, of a refusal of what the organism makes the body undergo. Not regression at all, but involution, involuted body' (Deleuze 1987: 110). Anorexia is therefore an experimentation with the emancipatory invention of a body that would not subject us to its demands.

It is also a politics of betrayal of natural hunger. Anorexics 'betray hunger, because hunger tricks them by making them subject to the organism' (Deleuze 1987: 110). Not to eat when the organs are hungry is to overcome the demands of specific organs in order to reach the fullness – immanence – of the body; it means forcing the organs to live without expectations and thus to become ascetic. Anorexia is therefore a praxis of asceticism.

The asceticism Deleuze has in mind – making the body lighter, while maintaining its materiality – aims to replace extensive quantities with intensive qualities of lightness and fastness. The anorexic experiments with becoming ever lighter so that in moving faster she turns extensions into intensities or pure affects. But to transform extensions (of organs) into intensities (of affection) is also to negate the limitations formed by organs and to produce a body made of alterations. Such a body, Deleuze suggests, is a rhythm of affects, intervals and appearance of new affects. The anorexic thus experiments with the affects of 'void' and 'fullness:' 'The anorexic consists of a body without organs, with voids and fullnesses. The alternation of stuffing and emptying: anorexic feasts, the imbibings of fizzy drinks. We should not even talk about alternation: void and fullness are like two demarcations of intensity; the point is always to float in one's own body' (Deleuze 1987). The anorexic is an inventor of a light and liquid body.

However, the anorexic betrays not only hunger (by eating irregularly, for instance) but also food, by never eating those large assemblages commonly called meals. What is more, she is experimenting with the possibility of eating that would be neither carnivorous nor involve eating 'fresh' life. She tries to find out whether it is possible to live on something without necessarily killing any 'body.' In so resisting the consumption of other bodies – and it is here that we see how anorexia becomes political – the anorexic resists the idea of being consumed by them: 'Anorexia is a political system, a micro-politics: to escape from the norm of consumption in order not to be an object of consumption oneself' (Deleuze 1987: 110). The anorexic eats bits and pieces, takes mouthfuls or sips, steals crumbs after the dinner is over, takes little bites from somebody else's plate, lives on the leftovers: 'I'm starving,' she says, grabbing two 'slimming yoghurts' (Deleuze 1987: 111). In other words, she assembles her body by collecting the particles of what has already been eaten. She composes her body out of already inorganic bodies in order to give herself a body that is equally inorganic. 'Her goal is to wrest particles from food, minute particles with which she will be able to create her void as well as her fullness, depending on whether she gives them out or receives them' (Deleuze 1987: 110).

Doing Cooking

The anorexic politics of tricking food by assembling a meal out of crumbs can become particularly subversive if she develops a taste for cooking; for then, as Deleuze says, she will turn 'consumption against itself: she will often be a cook, a peripatetic cook, who will make something for others to eat, or else she will like being at the table either without eating, or else multiplying the absorption of little things, of little substances' (Deleuze 1987: 110). The peripatetic cook turns consumption against itself because she does not let herself be consumed by the consuming. Everything is prepared for consumption and yet consumption does not occur since peripatetic cooking is precisely about enjoying the process of preparation without devouring its result; the anorexic is thus not entrapped by cooking for she does not eat what is cooked.

In *The Practice of Everyday Life* Luce Giard calls this praxis of cooking 'doing cooking' in contrast to simple 'cooking.' Doing cooking has nothing to do with eating what one has cooked:

> I discovered bit by bit not the pleasure of eating good meals, but that of manipulating raw material, of organising, combining, modifying, and inventing. I learned the tranquil joy of anticipated hospitality, when one prepares a meal to share with friends in the same way in which one composes a party tune or draws: with moving hands, careful fingers, the whole body inhabited with the rhythm of working, and the mind awakening, freed from its own ponderousness, flitting from idea to memory, finally seizing on a certain chain of thought, and then modulating this tattered writing once again. Thus, surreptitiously and without suspecting it, I had been invested with the secret, tenacious pleasure of *doing-cooking*. (Certeau, Giard and Mayol 1998: 153)

Doing-cooking is thus a version of the process of composing a tune or drawing. It is the art of making a body, reorganising particles, reassembling them, and doing so through the repetition and difference of rhythms and motions of one's own body. But it is also about inventing a spiritual intensive body, since the motion of body gives rise to the chain of thought which one inhabits rhythmically in order to move the mind. Doing-cooking is thus not only about tactile joy but about making hand and thought indistinguishable, about 'seizing on a ... thought' that would fall in with the rhythm of the body, which then inscribes itself into a new body it is contracting ('modulating this tattered writing once again'). By inscribing its rhythm into the body of prepared food such cooking produces a textuality; it is not about eating but about writing and reading. In the words of a woman quoted by Luce Giard:

> When this became clear in my mind, it was already too late. It then became necessary to try to explain its nature, meaning, and manner to myself in the hopes of understanding why that particular pleasure seems so close to the 'pleasure of the text,' why I twine such tight kinship ties between the writing of gestures and that of words, and if one is free to establish, as I do, a kind of reciprocity between their respective production. (Certeau, Giard and Mayol 1998: 153)

Doing-cooking is therefore about writing a text and then enjoying reading it: watching other people eating it, without participating in the meal or participating peripatetically, as a spectator who is only passing by.

By eating little substances from the plates of others after they have finished eating, or by cooking and serving the food without eating it, anorexic politics not only betrays hunger and food but also the ideology of family meals. Anorexia, Deleuze suggests, should thus also be seen as a protest against family meals and the dynamics of love and power traversing them (Deleuze 1987: 110). By the same token, when the anorexic prepares food for her friends and then watches them eating she is refusing to believe that only the ritual of 'eating together' – the ritual of sharing the dead bodies of others – can bring us closer. Instead, peripatetic cooking – the process of creating a new body as the gift for the guest – is her way of hosting: 'tranquil joy of anticipated hospitality.'

Case Study: Kafka

Kafka's love story with Milena can be read as an experiment in non-eating (together), thus as an effort to come closer to another without eating with her or, more radically, without eating at all. Kafka worked at evading the universal law that one has to eat in order to live. Not only was he a vegetarian who found pleasure in contradicting his sanatorium neighbor according to whom 'a meat diet [was] absolutely essential' for mental work (Kafka 1953: 70), advocating the perverse common-sense idea that thinking depends on eating life. More radically, Kafka experiments with the anomalous possibility of living without eating at all: 'the eating which I resumed again today (yesterday I ate nothing)' (Kafka 1953: 40). If he sometimes eats, he explains, it is only because there is always that 'call for dinner,' the 'mother's call,' a plate in front of him that his mother put there, which always faces him with the circumstance that 'unfortunately' food 'wouldn't disappear from the plate save by being swallowed' (Kafka 1953: 126), whereas he would rather avoid swallowing (is it possible to live without swallowing others?). Similarly, he explains to Milena, he will eat while in the sanatorium only in order to be able to travel to Prague and Vienna to see her: 'on the ground floor of my building is, obligingly enough, a vegetarian restaurant where I'm eating, *not in order to eat* but to bring with me to Prague a certain amount of weight' (Kafka 1953: 61) – even though he realises that his economy, the fact that he takes a mouthful or two for love of the mother or lover, is non-economical since he is in fact trying to do away with that economy. Here is the secret of his politics of the body: to the torturous question so often asked by the members of his family – How much weight have you put on this time? – he wants to be able to answer not, 'I have put on or lost this or that much weight,' but 'And one is losing weight' (Kafka 1953: 70). Where there was an 'I' ('I lost weight') now there is 'one,' some body becoming lighter, an impersonal and inorganic body.

Such a body thus enters the outside of the law and becomes not a body that performs or fulfills tasks, obeys or demands, does or does not respond to calls (finally free from the 'call for dinner'), but one that approaches the joyful irresponsibility of lightness and freedom that Kafka's literary characters strove, always unsuccessfully, to achieve. This light body, Kafka explains, is alive, but belongs to no citizen of the world, for it is a non-trust worthy body:

> don't you know that only fat people are trustworthy? Only in these strong-walled vessels does everything get thoroughly cooked, only these capitalists of the airspace are, as far as it is possible for human beings, protected against worry and madness and are able to go calmly about their business, and they alone are, as someone once said, useful in the whole world as world-citizens, for in the North they warm and in the South they give shade. (Kafka 1953: 49)

In contrast to the citizens who eat, Kafka's body is so light that it is 'weak-walled' (becoming the body without organs), approaching the ecstasy of forms through trance-formation. It is the body of a lumpen-proletarian of the airspace that barely breaths, even though it is still alive, inhabiting the very boundary between life and death. Kafka sees it as a body that has become so small and imperceptible that it is 'incapable of dying,' even when 'the angel of death, the most beatific of all angels' comes and looks at it and calls it. It is a body become so light that it is incapable of sleeping: 'how could I have slept, since I, too light for sleep, circled around you...' (Kafka 1953: 45). The anomalous logic of Kafka's anorexic thinking suggests that sleeping requires a certain amount of weight: that one has to eat in order to dream. Sleep is possible only under the law of what Derrida calls 'carno-phallogocentrism,' the law of the carnivorous virility that constitutes the 'human' world: 'I would like to explain *carno-phallogocentrism*, even if this comes down to a sort of tautology or rather hetero-tautology as a priori synthesis... it suffices to take seriously the idealizing interiorization of the phallus and the necessity of its passage through the mouth, whether it's a matter of words or of things, of sentences, of daily bread or wine, of the tongue, the lips, or the breast of the other' (Derrida 1995: 280). But a body that does not swallow, breathe, sleep, dream or die, which is how Kafka wants his body, becomes an inorganic and living sensuality that, by falling outside the human, evades its 'carno-phallogocentrism.'

Kafka described the life of such a body in a series of his 1922 diary entries. Comparing his life to that of his bachelor uncle, he wrote: 'Both living the most unvarying lives, with no trace of any development, young to the end of your days ("well-preserved" is a better expression)'

(Kafka 1976: 403). A well-preserved life, an eternally young life, exists outside of time, or as an inorganic life of the body without organs. But it is not dead for being out of temporality; rather it is liberated from the self-mediation by which it could appropriate itself and set itself on the course of development. Kafka does not want to develop his life: 'I don't want to pursue any particular course of development.' It is easy to pursue paths, he suggests; for that it is enough to split oneself, 'it would be enough if I could exist alongside myself, it would even be enough if I could consider the spot on which I stand as some other spot' (Kafka 1976: 405). In other words, it would be enough to become a subject. But Kafka's subjectivity remains a hypothesis – 'if I could' – out of reach; his weakness is his inability to host a firm personal identity. As long as he remains incapable of self-mediation his life is without history (therefore outside of time), a life without genesis. It is a nameless life that feels without localising the feeling. Kafka described it as a hesitation that occurs before inhabiting a person: 'Hesitation before birth. If there is a transmigration of souls then I am not yet on the bottom rung. My life is a hesitation before birth' (Kafka 1976: 405).

Manners: The Body of the Cook-Model

A life without development is not in stasis; it does not follow the path of organic, linear progress and escapes the connection between cause and effect, but it still has its motions and intensities. Located outside genealogy, historical formation and the organism, it wants to invent a different logic and different signifiers, to construe signs that would not be representative of something, but be bodies in themselves. The anorexic thus opposes symbolics to cartography, since her body is not the symbol of a lack of food, of psychic disorder, or of a disturbance of desire, but is instead, a chart of newly invented signs which are its very matter. As an anomalous chart of signs that defy symbolics the anorexic embodies a negation of the differences between genus and species or between genders. The anorexic is neither masculine nor feminine but – contrary to such a distinction – a process of becoming a woman, the 'woman-becoming of every anorexic' (Deleuze 1987: 110).

Nor is the anorexic's inorganic body an asexual one: 'There is a whole plane of construction of the anorexic, making oneself an anorganic body (which does not mean asexual: on the contrary...).' It is, as I have suggested, about the production of certain fluxes and its sexuality will be an exercise in the fusion of those fluxes: fluxes of food (crumbs, tiny substances); fluxes of liquids (the imbibing of fizzy drinks); fluxes of abstinence or consumption; fluxes of signifiers that disrupt genealogy. Deleuze suggests that in anorexia all these fluxes mix, get assembled and reassembled in order finally, to be, combined with the fluxes of clothes: 'The case of anorexia. It is a question of food fluxes, but combined with other fluxes, clothes fluxes, for example (specifically anorexic elegance)' (Deleuze 1987: 110). Thus, not only can it happen that the anorexic is a peripatetic cook; she will also often be a model: 'She will often be a model – she will often be a cook . . . Cook-model, a mixture that can only exist in this assemblage, this system, and which will be dissolved in different ones' (Deleuze 1987: 110). Deleuze thus obviously wants to do away with the idea that models are simply an effect of the socially imposed image of the body. According to this misconception, the body of the model would be fashioned after the already existing image of a perfect female body, which is to say as a regulative representation that imposes the norm of the erotic body. Such an image would be a phantasmatic vehicle aimed at disciplining female bodies, making them uniform according to a presupposed, but equally phantasmatic masculine desire. Models would thus be an image of the feminine body that responds to masculine desire. The image of the model, then, enables both the circulation of socially desirable bodies and the masculine desire that controls feminine bodies. But such an interpretation is itself caught in the ideology of two sexes, Deleuze suggests, since in supposing that the masculine fashions the feminine it itself fantasises the existence of a universal masculine desire. However, desires are neither masculine nor feminine but always singular, assemblages of various masculine, feminine, vegetable, animal and inorganic components. And it is the particular singularity or admixture of those components that produces the specificity of anorexic desire.

To 'have' an anorexic cook-model body is precisely to experiment with its fashioning by mixing fluxes of food with fluxes of clothes, which will turn the body into a texture of specifically anorexic signifiers. For that reason the question of fashion becomes so important for the anorexic. Here, Deleuze wants to avoid another widespread prejudice. Anorexic elegance, he will claim, is not about consuming – having things that everybody has – but rather about existing in a mode that subverts the difference between genus and species. It tries to find its way out of the opposition between being and non-being by entering the existence of becoming or, more precisely, of manners. Anorexic elegance, then, is about modal existence, and its signifying logic is similarly one of manners. The formula of anorexic elegance, therefore, is not fashion and consumption but fashion and manners or style ('style . . . a 'mode of life' [Deleuze, 1987: 3]).

Manners are the operators of modal logic; based on adjectives and infinite verbs modal logic is the force of what Deleuze calls 'differentiating being,' itself a motion made of a 'plurality of centers,' or becomings. As the logic of multiplicity without substance, modal logic is one of intensities – of the 'being of the sensible' (Deleuze 1994: 57) – and it is with that being that the cook-model experiments. The formulaic version of modal being – "the same returns not, save to bring the different' – is something Deleuze takes from Benjamin Blood's *Anesthetic Revelation*, quoted by William James. Deleuze also elaborates modal being through James' radical empiricism, which owes a great deal not only to Blood but also to Emerson. It is therefore not surprising that the logic of manners, and by extension of fashion, which Deleuze seeks to elaborate, leads to the American philosophers whose thinking was nothing if not a fascinating effort to articulate a manneristic ontology. The radicality introduced by these thinkers into the Western understanding of manners, and the kind of body that is at stake in the manneristic body of the cook-model, become evident once one examines the logic proposed by Emerson and James, which is echoed by Deleuze in *Difference and Repetition*.

Manners, says Emerson, are not rituals: 'The maiden at her first ball, the country-man at a city dinner, believes that there is a ritual according to which every act and compliment must be performed, or the failing party must be cast out of this presence. Later, they learn that good sense and character make their own forms every moment' (Emerson 1996: 520). Manners are opposed to rituals because they are opposed to forms: 'For there is nothing settled in manners, but the laws of behavior yield to the energy of the individual' (Emerson 1996: 519). Emerson, thus elaborates a novel concept of manners that works against the etymology of the word. For manners (from *manere, maniere*) etymologically refer to what is accustomed or ritualised. Colloquially understood, then, the word refers to our habitual ways of behavior, to a usual form of acting. By defining manners as what unsettles the habitual – what Benjamin Blood, cited by Deleuze, refers to as the 'wild' (Deleuze 1994: 57) – Emerson signals that they are a way of being that goes against not only our 'natural' needs (our so-called 'first nature') but also against our habits ('second nature'). The manneristic way of life, he implies, is thus a 'technology of the self,' which could be determined as the praxis of ridding us of a habit. Manners become a painful exercise that forces one to re-shape one's identity while declining from relying on anything firm or formed. Manners are differentiating processes before the establishment of differences, what Deleuze would come to call 'lines of flight.'

Manners are unsettling because, says Emerson, they are the effect of a momentous 'fine perception' (Emerson 1996: 523) that registers what passes as imperceptible for everybody else. They belong to what he calls 'the energy' of the individual, resulting from motions that escape the perception of the 'I;' they happen to the I, they are never designed by it. In contriving themselves as differences produced by life rather than by a reflective self they lead the self to abandon its habits. And since manners force the 'I' in us to yield to the laws of behavior that constitute it, by the same token they force the I to give up on itself; they are the expression of a life freed from the obstacles of personhood: 'Manners aim to facilitate life, to get rid of impediments, and bring the man pure to energize. They aid our dealing and conversation, as a railway aids traveling, by getting rid of all avoidable obstructions of the road, and leaving nothing to be conquered but pure space' (Emerson 1996: 517). Manners do not exist as 'mine' but are possible only as the effect of the relation that connects impersonal lives. They are processual yet a-temporal, negating the 'I' that always remains conditioned by time. Manners are a purely exterior relation that belongs to nobody, styles in sheer space ('leaving nothing to be conquered but pure space'). For that reason they amount to a most profound criticism of western ontology, subverting the distinction between being and non-being. They are, but they are 'nobody's,' 'points and fences disappear,' Emerson says, there is only flying and fleeing. They therefore 'introduce' being – since they are – but in such a way that nothing particular can be ascribed to that being, neither substance nor essence. When Deleuze talks about anorexic elegance and style, and when he specifies style to be a mode or manner of life, he is evoking this idea of manneristic living as an experiment in the impersonal, in the diminution of the 'I' that gives way to an intensified life. It is precisely with such a way of being that the anorexic-model conducts its experiments.

To return to Deleuze via Emerson once more, the 'style' this 'non-individual' singularity is produced precisely by fashion. In its objectless existence, fashion becomes the profound enactment of manneristic existence: 'the objects of fashion may be frivolous, or fashion may be objectless, but the nature of this union and selection can be neither frivolous nor accidental' (Emerson 1996: 519). To hold that fashion is objectless is to suggest that it does not signify or represent anything; it is not an idea of a body that a subject wants to convey to another subject. Rather, it is the materiality of its own presence; it is the body fashioned. Fashion crafts the body in such a way that it mutates and appears in its outsideness, manifesting itself on the surface; in becoming inorganic the body becomes its clothes. But since the disappearance of the organic body is, in fact, the vanishing of the self – for self is located in the image of its own body – fashion becomes the force of absorption of the self into itself; by negating both body and self it produces an assemblage of subjectless-objectless clothes in motion. The radicalism of experimentation with fashion lies, then, in the fact that the prosthetic body contrived of clothes becomes the only body there is. Fashion is thus the operation through which the organic body and its self takes off into inorganic flight.

It is only by means of Emerson's identification of fashionable manners with the occurrence of a rhythmical and 'musical nature' (Emerson 1996: 529) or with a 'more transparent atmosphere,' that one can understand Deleuze's sparse remarks on anorexic elegance and the body of the model. Manners are atmospheric because they are a purely external relation, existing in the outside as a selfless and objectless 'something.' They move impersonally through the bodies of others, traversing their perceptions and so affecting them. Manners – styles, modes – therefore have the nature of a Deleuzian event.

The event is what Deleuze refers to as the happening – an almost imperceptible occurrence – of *something*; something without any representable identity and hence without sufficient reason. An event, therefore, always occurs as 'something that happens' and not as a 'this' or 'that' that is going on (Beckett gave perhaps its most precise formulation in saying 'something is taking its course' [Beckett 1958: 32]). And because this happening of something cannot be represented or identified, it happens to no one. Once the event is identified it has already taken place; identification of it comes only in retrospect. But while it is happening it is the only entity there is, non-appropriated, unnamed, unimagined, just 'something' taking its course. Entities are thus neither things nor objects, neither thoughts nor concepts, but purely external relations or manners. The reverse holds too: only manners are events since, according to Deleuze's equation 'true Entities are events, not concepts.... ENTITY = EVENT; it is a terror, but also great joy (Deleuze 1987: 66).' The terror derives from an annihilation of the 'I', but it is also the great joy of no one caused by something since the joy is never personalised or appropriated (the gestures that transform joy into the pleasure of the subject). It is an impersonal excitement of little motions that change the direction or rhythm of all perceptions; Deleuze compares it to the breeze in a desert, or else to 'small,' 'delicate' things: 'Making an event – however small – is the most delicate thing in the world: the opposite of making a drama or making a story' (Deleuze 1987: 66). Again, this delicate thing is a terror because it inflicts the suffering of constant displacement without the comfort of reterritorialisation (becoming is unsettling, there is nothing pleasurable about becomings); and it is joy because the terror of slight dislocations – the feeling that one is never quite in one's place – brings with an 'atmospheric variation,' ushering in the fresh air that enables breathing. As Deleuze says, echoing Emerson: 'Loving those who are like this: when they enter a room they are not persons, characters or subjects, but an atmospheric variation, a change of hue, an imperceptible molecule, a discrete population, a fog or a cloud of droplets. Everything has really changed' (Deleuze 1987: 66).

The anorexic model experiments precisely with such real changes in the atmosphere, with events. In his 'Homage to Fanny' Deleuze specifies that anorexic experimentation works not only with clothes – a body becoming an inorganic patchwork, a design, a style – but also with variations and alternations of stuffing and emptying, ever so slight (Deleuze 1987: 110). When an anorexic cat-model enters the room what actually walks in is not a person, character or a subject, but 'a discrete population' of clothes, voids and ways of walking – a manner – whose delicate being will cause an atmospheric variation.

Fashion and Radical Empiricism

It was William James who, in his *Psychology: Briefer Course,* drew radical consequences from Emerson's hints about manners and fashion. In chapter XII, on 'The Self,' James differentiated among the material, social and spiritual Me, identifying the body as the inner core of the material selfhood:

> The *body* is the innermost part of the material me in each of us ... The clothes come next. The old saying that the human person is composed of three parts – soul, body and clothes – is more than a joke. We so appropriate our clothes and identify ourselves with them that there are few of us who, if asked to choose between having a beautiful body clad in raiment perpetually shabby and unclean, and having an ugly and blemished form always spotlessly attired, would not hesitate a moment before making a decisive reply. (James 1992: 175)

The clear distinction between body and clothes – body comes first, the clothes next – is thus made only in order to be blurred. Since people always prefer nice clothes and an ugly body to a beautiful body and bad clothes, James will come to reverse the prioritisation of his initial distinction and claim priority for clothes. Clothes come before the body because the self identifies with them more intensely than with its body, thus in fact turning the clothes into the body, literally or materially, producing the body out of inorganic artificial textures. The innermost core of the material self is thus its clothes. But this inversion doesn't affect only the material self; in order for clothes to morph into the material self, what James calls the 'spiritual me' – the self 'proper' as it were – has to identify with them and so appropriate them as its own body. Not only, then, do clothes become the body, but through the process of identification they enter the spiritual me. The innermost core of the spiritual turns out to be textile. The scandal of the self that James signals, thus lies in the spiritual's contrivance as inorganic exteriority. The logic of James' argument is similar to Emerson's since here, too, through its identification with clothes, the object (the body) is removed, and fashion enters the spiritual self, absorbing it into an assemblage of selfless clothes.

If this reading seems idiosyncratic one should remember that after describing various 'states of consciousness,' (attention, conception, discrimination, emotion and will) James added an 'Epilogue' to the *Course* that destabilised the existence of the 'I' and blurred distinctions among 'interiority,' spirituality, personality and exteriority. In fact, he wrote there that the psychology he himself had outlined was a 'mere provisional statement from a popular and prejudiced point of view' (James 1992: 432), based on the premise of an interiority whose existence could not be proven. The real question, the question of the existence of the 'I' and the 'states of consciousness,' remained for him disturbingly open, for everything pointed to its non-existence:

> States of consciousness themselves are not verifiable facts.... Neither common-sense, nor psychology so far as it has yet been written, has ever doubted that the states of consciousness which that science studies are immediate data of experience. 'Things' have been doubted, but thoughts and feelings have never been doubted. The outer world, but never the inner world, has been denied.... Yet I must confess that for my part I cannot feel sure of this conclusion. Whenever I try to become sensible of my thinking activity as such, what I catch is some bodily fact, an impression coming from my brow, or head, or throat, or nose. It seems as if consciousness as an inner activity were rather a *postulate* than a sensibly given fact. (James 1992: 432)

This conclusion supports my reading of James' chapter on clothes and the Self. In contrast to the metaphysical voices dismissing the external as a mere superfluous accident, James claims exteriority to be the only thing there is; the 'I' with its apparatus of interiority and spirituality is only a fragile hypothesis, a postulate effected by our 'will to believe' in it, whereas it is in fact impossible to sense, feel or think. There is, thus, only a multiplicity of points and lines, whose intensity gives them a certain extension that composes an exteriority, an exteriority that has to be called pure as it depends on no interiority. The is why the only sustainable hypothesis is that of an exterior that thinks and affects itself, what James called 'radical empiricism.' The lines of motion of these thought-affects constitute the living world, are its cartography.

The Deleuzian anorexic cook-model, I am suggesting, is in those terms a radical empiricist. Her experimenting with fashion is guided by a weakening of the 'will to believe in the 'I,'' since her acts are directed against the prejudice of its existence. She experiments with becoming a 'multiple exteriority,' whose body and self are assembled from the artificial materials of clothes and their motion. In that way she invents a body transformed into the lines of a specific functioning: the motion of clothes, the void of the body becoming the rhythm of walking, and the walk – the 'cat walk' – turning the rhythm of the walk into an anorexic becoming animal. As Deleuze suggests, such a body works, but loses both its organic and its social functionality. Because her body is neither objectivised – but, to the contrary, is made objectless – nor subjectivised – since she is impersonal – it escapes the demands the social wants to impose on it. Its functioning renders social codes inoperative. That is why Deleuze specifies anorexia as a micro-political rebellion. Far from being an effect of obedience to consumer neurosis, the anorexic experimentation is: 'a feminine protest, from a woman who wants to have a functioning of the body and not simply organic and social functions which make her dependent' (Deleuze 1987: 110).

Only from the perspective of the modeling of the anorexic body can the question of a specifically anorexic elegance be addressed. What perhaps remains to be understood is Deleuze's identification of the 'wholly trinity' of anorexic elegance: Virginia Woolf, Murnau, Kay Kendall.

Waves, Cardigans and Facelessness

Virginia Woolf figures prominently in the anorexic cartography because of the ways in which she turns assemblages of things – words, clothes, bodies – into the motion of waves. Waves are passages, the paradoxical existence of a non-being, with which the anorexic also experiments. As Deleuze and Guattari explain:

> Waves are vibrations, shifting borderlines inscribed on the plane as so many abstractions... In *The Waves*, Virginia Woolf – who made all of her life and

work a passage, a becoming, all kinds of becomings between ages, sexes, elements, and kingdoms – intermingles seven characters, Bernard, Neville, Louis, Jinny, Rhoda, Suzanne, and Percival. But each of these characters, with his or her name, its individuality, designates a multiplicity (for example, Bernard and the school of fish). Each is simultaneously in this multiplicity and at its edge, and crosses over into the others.... Each advances like a wave, but on the plane of consistency they are a single abstract Wave whose vibration propagates following a line of flight or deterritorialization traversing the entire plane. (Deleuze and Guatarri 1988: 252)

A wave, then, is this multiple individuality that at the same time resides within itself, at the edge separating it from other bodies, and crosses over into those bodies; no longer itself, but nothing definitive yet, leaving itself while arriving only at motion, a motion engaged simultaneously in various alliances.

Take the example of Rhoda. She herself signals an anorexic pragmatics by experimenting with the lightness of the body, with its becoming ever thinner, so she can become imperceptible and thus enter Susan, Jinny or Bernard, but never to stay Rhoda or become her again. She wants to have a body that can 'fall through the thin sheet now;' she wants to be able to 'spread my body on this frail mattress and hang suspended.' She wants to become so light that her body will be turned into a ray of light and finally fly over the body of Earth, never again pressured by the force of gravitation: 'I am above the earth now... All is soft, and bending.... Out of me now my mind can pour... heap themselves on me; they sweep me between their great shoulders; I am turned; I am tumbled; I am stretched, among these long lights, these long waves, these endless paths, with people pursuing, pursuing' (Woolf 1959: 28).

Rhoda's gesture is one of protest, protest against a world made of people 'pursuing, pursuing,' or functioning, functioning, in order to become alive, a dysfunctional multiple wave. But she cannot flee and fly, without becoming faceless. In fact, she is becoming faceless in order to be able to inhabit faces, not only Susan's or Jinny's, but those of all nameless women, and thus in order to realise the paradox of assuming the face of *a* woman, an impersonal, unknown face: 'But I attach myself only to names and faces; and hoard them like amulets against disaster. I choose out across the hall some unknown face and can hardly drink my tea when she whose name I do not know sits opposite. I choke. I am rocked from side to side by the violence of my emotion' (ibid.: 43). The anorexic living on tea chokes on it, interrupting its liquid flux, leaving that line and moving into an impersonal assemblage composed of unknown faces. It is that very moving in and out that puts her on the line of intense rocking, that of 'the violence of my emotion.'

But Rhoda knows that this becoming a 'rocking' emotion by passage through names and bodies is also related to becoming other women's clothes. As she explains, it's not only a matter of having Jinny's stockings or Susan's skirts, but also about wearing stockings the way Jinny does, wearing skirts the way Susan does; thus, it is about combining various women's styles, picking up on the way they wear their clothes: 'See now with what extraordinary certainty Jinny pulls on her stockings' (Woolf 1959: 28). To wear the clothes of women in the multiple ways they wore them is to experiment in composing variable abstract planes of signs, to assemble impersonal styles into new modes of immanence; but to do so is also to compose a whole cartography of diverse histories – to spatialise time – since Rhoda's assemblages crystalise the whole history of women's clothing, moving and gesturing in a moment of almost perfect composition, the moment of being rocked from 'side to side.'

Such is the temporality of anorexic elegance: time embedded in a place in space and appearing out of it; the whole history of a body swallowed by the now of a thing. That is how I read Virginia Woolf's sentence quoted by Deleuze and Guattari as a formulaic expression of the organic stepping over the threshold of the inorganic: 'The thin dog is running in the road, this dog is the road' (Deleuze and Guattari 1992: 263). Similarly, the thin Rhoda is walking in everybody's clothes, Rhoda is those clothes. This anorexic becoming of an impersonal place enacts the production of feeling spread out through space, in a world where humans become a summer and plants morph into an afternoon: 'That is how we need to feel. Spatiotemporal relations, determinations, are not predicates of the thing but dimensions of multiplicities... We are all five o'clock in the evening, or another hour, or rather two hours simultaneously, the optimal and the pessimal, noon-midnight, but distributed in a variable fashion. The plane of consistency contains only haecceities, along intersecting lines. Forms and subjects are not of that world' (Deleuze and Guattari 1992: 263). Rhoda's clothes embody such a haecceity; they represent not other women and their habits or sexuality, but the line of motion of a woman, the trajectory of movement of an abstract and impersonal woman. Her clothes are, therefore, not symbolic; rather, her motion outlines a chart: 'A cartography and never a symbolics.' The hope of the anorexic-model is that her abstraction – her clothes produced as the perfect combination of signs signifying nothing and calling for nothing – will outline a chart of her movement; her hope is that she will become a cartography taking an impersonal walk and constructing an altogether different London, with neither streets nor people but only fleeting stares or glares.

Virginia Woolf experimented thus: long cardigans, hair pulled back, everything working towards becoming ever longer and thinner, only a curve, a line taking a walk:

> Virginia Woolf's walk through the crowd, among the taxis. Taking a walk is a haecceity; never again will Mrs. Dalloway say to herself, 'I am this, I am that, he is this, he is that.' And 'She felt very young: at the same time unspeakably aged. She sliced like a knife through everything; at the same time was outside, looking on... She always had the feeling that it was very, very dangerous to live even one day. Haecceity, fog, glare.' (Deleuze and Guattari 1992: 263)

Or, as Deleuze also suggests, shadows and contrasts.

The Dynamic Sublime and the Question of Make-up

If Virginia Woolf stands in the trinity of anorexic elegance for becoming the clothes of the body, Murnau stands for becoming the shadow of the face. For it was Murnau, says Deleuze, who broke with the principles of organic composition without substituting for them the 'mechanics of the quantity of movement in the solid or the fluid.' Instead, there is 'a dark, swampy life into which everything plunges, whether chopped up by shadows or plunged into mists. *The non-organic life of things,* a frightful life, which is oblivious to the wisdom and limits of the organism, is the first principle of Expressionism' (Deleuze 1986: 50–1). Such a life is frightful only from the perspective of the organic, which insists on the fundamental difference between 'natural' and 'artificial,' believing that confusing the two brings life into the dangerous vicinity of death. That is why the body of the anorexic model transformed into clothes, as well as her face contrived by make-up, represents for the organic point of view an artificiality that negates the 'depth' of the face, announcing prosthetic death. However, Murnau's experiment – and this is why the anorexic likes him – far from being about death, is in fact about expanding life into the 'inorganic,' making things tremble by putting everything in motion:

> From this point of view natural substances and artificial creations, candelabras and trees, turbine and sun are no longer any different. A wall which is alive is dreadful; but utensils, furniture, houses and their roofs also lean, crowd around, lie in wait, or pounce. Shadows of houses pursue the man running along the street. In all these cases, it is not the mechanical which is opposed to the organic: it is the vital as potent pre-organic germinality,

common to the animate and the inanimate, to a matter which raises itself
to the point of life, and to a life which spreads itself through all matter.
(Deleuze 1986: 50–1)

The attempt to reach the potent pre-organic vitality shared by animate
and inanimate alike, the life that precedes and comes after any death,
is what drives Murnau's invention of 'facelessness.' Take the anorexic
Nosferatu as a case in point. His pale face signifies lifelessness and turns
him into a phantom only from a perspective such as the Freudian, which
privileges death over life, from the vantage which, as Deleuze notoriously
put it, operates according to the 'white wall, black hole' distinction,
and which thus functions in the organic terms of a difference between
living subject and mortified object. Deleuze's point is that the 'white
wall, black hole' distinction is rendered inoperative by Nosferatu, who
in fact has no face at all, not even a 'Gothic' face of paleness against
a dark background. To think of the Gothic (for example, fashion) as
an insistence on black (clothes) versus white (face); or to think of a
Gothic face as the difference between its whiteness and an intensely red
lipstick, is to ignore that Gothic esthetics works not with faces at all,
but rather with the convulsions that contrive formlessness. Murnau's or
Worringer's invocation of the Gothic is thus driven by the

> opposition of vital force (*élan vital*) to organic representation, invoking the
> 'Gothic or Northern' decorative line, a broken line which forms no contour
> by which form and background might be distinguished, but passes in a zigzag
> between things, sometimes drawing them into a bottomlessness in which it
> loses itself, sometimes whirling them in a formlessness into which it veers in
> a 'disorderly convulsion'. (Deleuze 1986: 50–1)

The annulled distinction between form and background suggests that
broken lines are not drawn in an already existing space of forms – which
alone is what makes faces possible – but within the logic of a specifically
'Gothic geometry ... [which] constructs space instead of describing it.'
The point is therefore not to try to recognise forms but to follow the
points of their intersection, where there occur the blurred contrasts of
shadows or motions of formless colors.

Within such a visuality for example, the intersection of black and blue
will constitute not a form but a degree of darkened white in contrast to
a 'toned down' black:

> It is as though two degrees were apprehended in an instant, points of
> accumulation which would correspond to the upsurge of colour in Goethe's
> theory: blue as lightened black, yellow as darkened white.... Goethe
> explained precisely that the two fundamental colours – yellow and blue

as degrees – were grasped in a *movement of intensification*, which was accompanied in both cases by a reddish reflection. (Deleuze 1986: 52)

In contradistinction to a Newtonian optics based on forms, Murnau follows Goethe's optics of the intense motions of colors, which transcend form. For that reason that it would be wrong to call Nosferatu a dead face, or a mask made of intensely white foundation contrasted with red lipstick playing the role of the black. If Nosferatu is faceless, it is because the intensity of the contrast between white and black is transformed into a presentation of pure colors. What one sees is precisely the imperceptible, or intensity:

> In Murnau, in particular, *Nosferatu* does not merely pass through all the spects of chiaroscuro, of back-lighting and of the non-organic life of shadows, he does not merely produce all the moments of a reddish reflection, but he reaches a climax when a powerful light (a pure red) isolates him from his shadowy background, making him burst forth from an even more direct bottomlessness, giving him an aura of omnipotence which goes beyond his two dimensional form. (Deleuze 1986: 53)

The pale face of the anorexic-model, her red lipstick and black clothes, are not about the Gothic trivially understood as the representation of 'dark forces' invoked by insistence on the sharp forms of the body, face, lips or eyes. Rather, if the anorexic appreciates Murnau, it is because she has learned his lesson: how to produce a motion of pure colors at the point of intersection of black, white, yellow, blue and red. Anorexic elegance, therefore, works not on a contrast of white and black but on the point of their intersection – shades and shadows – where blue or yellow appear. The lipstick on the anorexic face does not delineate those lips against the backdrop of that face but casts a reflection of red on white, blue or black, producing an atmosphere of pure redness, the force of pure intensity. What is more, her face does not have lips, eyes, jaws or nose. It is paleness or whiteness becoming red, the intensification of whiteness into the blazing red. Thus she experiments in the same way as Murnau's expressionism, trying to turn the face into a formless intensity or, differently, into a certain type of the sublime: 'Kant distinguished two kinds of Sublime, mathematical and dynamic, the immense and the powerful, the measureless and the formless. Both had the property of decomposing organic composition, the first by going beyond it, the second by breaking it' (Deleuze 1986: 53). But in contrast to the mathematical sublime, in which 'the extensive unit of measurement changes so much that the imagination is no longer able to comprehend it,' anorexic elegance or the 'Murnau experiment' produces the dynamic sublime:

> In the dynamic sublime, it is intensity which is raised to such a power that it dazzles or annihilates our organic being, strikes terror into it, but arouses a thinking faculty by which we feel superior to that which annihilates us, to discover in us a supra-organic spirit which dominates the whole inorganic life of things: then we lose our fear, knowing that our spiritual 'destination' is truly invincible. (Deleuze 1986: 53)

Thus, the anorexic-model works with pure terror, namely with what annihilates us. But she does that because it is, counterintuitively, through that terror, through the intensity of the annihilation of the organic, that she acquires the power to lose her fear while reaching and feeling pure life.

However, the body become the motion of clothes and impersonal walks, assuming the anomalous position of being at the same time inside and outside (Virginia Woolf); and the annihilation of the face, its turning into the process of intensification of colors, its becoming atmosphere (Murnau) constitute only two components of anorexic elegance. What is still needed is the power to turn the walks, the motions, the intensities and the terror of annihilation, into the joy of doing it time and again, thus reinventing life. That is the function fulfilled by Kay Kendall in the anorexic trinity.

Les Girls

It was Kay Kendall who invented the art of imperceptible glamour. She mixed little black dresses and big black hats with white pearls and a lot of fur (Murnau's esthetics), combining them with her long, thin body, moving slowly in order to remain imperceptible. The *Star Archive* claims that 'she hasn't become the same sort of cult figure that say Dean or Monroe became, but then she was far too sensible for that sort of nonsense,' since their glamour was molar. Instead, Kay Kendall entered the becoming of a girl. The little dancing girl (she was a dancer in the chorus at the Palladium by the time she was twelve) became the trumpet player (*Genevieve*) who, thanks to Vincent Minnelli, then became *The Reluctant Debutante*, a dizzy socialite following the rhythm of music and fizzy drinks, finally merging with Cukor's *Les Girls*, becoming one of the girls, a girl, many girls, the French-English-American mixture of accents, motions, languages and tastes. The anorexic goal was thus realised in this reluctant becoming a girl of the woman.

Importantly, most film encyclopedias and archives refer to Kendall's various roles as one, and speak of her 'screen persona' as if the various girls she played or was became one. But that oneness doesn't contradict the differences among Kendall's performances. For what those film scholars refer to as Kendall's 'persona' is, in fact, a mode of the impersonal. For they write as if of an atmosphere composed of unstable mixtures of 'fifties poise,' 'glamour,' 'sensuality,' 'elegance,' and a particular way of walking that bordered on dancing. Thus Kendall managed to merge varieties of screen persons into what Deleuze and Guattari called the 'aesthetic figure':

> Aesthetic figures, and the style that creates them, have nothing to do with rhetoric. They are sensations: percepts and affects, landscapes and faces, visions and becoming. But is not the philosophical concept defined by becoming, and almost in the same terms? Still, aesthetic figures are not the same as conceptual personae. It may be that they pass into one another, in either direction, like Igitur or Zarathustra, but this is insofar as there are sensations of concepts and concepts of sensations. It is not the same becoming. Sensory becoming is the action by which something or someone is ceaselessly becoming-other (while continuing to be what they are), sunflower or Ahab... Conceptual becoming is heterogeneity grasped in an absolute form; sensory becoming is otherness caught in the matter of expression. (Deleuze and Guattari 1994b: 177)

The aesthetic 'persona' thus becomes an impersonal proliferation of percepts and affects caught in the matter of expression such that the expression becomes the matter itself; the immaterial expression.

Style is the vehicle of this becoming a pure expression of percepts, as Deleuze specifies. The aesthetic 'persona' is the effect of styles, which 'are not constructions, any more than are modes of life.' As becomings 'they are the thing which is the most imperceptible, they are acts which can only be contained in a life and expressed in a style.' Becoming style, as the expression of percept and affects, is not an effect of something or somebody: 'There is nothing to understand, nothing to interpret' (Deleuze 1987: 4). There is nobody behind the style since style is not an expression of somebody's desires, nightmares or fantasies. Rather, it is the pure, impersonal motion of affects. Kay Kendall, therefore, is not a glamorous person but the atmosphere of glamour from which everything personal has vanished. The final goal of anorexic experimentation is to become such an aesthetic 'persona,' the sensory becoming of otherness that affects by the force of percepts and overwhelms by the sheer power of assemblages of hats, pearls, little black dresses and a touch of a perfume. By reaching towards impersonal life the anorexic turns her body-clothes into an aesthetic persona in the same way that she turns food into abstract textuality and enacts a sort of enjoyment in the text.

The Enthusiast

The fact that the anorexic tends towards the dynamic sublime, and that her experimentation represents the devastation of the personal self, finally explains what might be understood as Deleuze's principal claim about anorexia, that 'anorexics are enthusiasts.'

A story related by De Certeau places the anorexic-enthusiast not only at the very origin of institutionalised Christianity but interprets her experimentation along the lines of Deleuze's thesis, as a micro-politics directed both against the Father and the ideal of the Virgin Mother, in short, against the symbolic field. De Certeau quotes this passage from *Lausiac History*:

> In this monastery there was a virgin who pretended to be mad, possessed by a demon. The others became so disgusted with her that no one ate with her, which she preferred. Wandering through the kitchen, she would render any service. She was, as they say, the sponge of the monastery. In reality, she was accomplishing what is written: 'If someone intends to be wise among us in this life, let him become a fool to become wise.' She had tied a rag around her head – all the others are shaven and wear hoods – and it is in that attire that she performed her duties. Of the four hundred [sisters], not one ever saw her chew anything during the years of her life; she never sat at table; she never broke bread with the others. She was happy with the crumbs she wiped up and the water from the pots and pans she scoured, without offending anyone, without murmuring, without speaking little or much, though she was beaten with blows, insulted, laden with curses, and treated with disgust. (De Certeau 1992: 34–5)

Without going into de Certeau's analysis of the specifically enthusiastic 'logic' of thinking, which thinks without the object, I quote his conclusion to establish a fundamental connection between anorexia and becoming a woman:

> A woman, then. She doesn't leave the kitchen. She doesn't leave off *being* something that has to do with the crumbs and leftovers of food. She makes her body from them. She maintains herself by being nothing but this abject point, the 'nothing' that puts people off... Around her hair, a dishrag. No discontinuity between her and this refuse: she doesn't 'chew'; nothing separates her body from the offal. She is what is left over, without end, infinite. The opposite of the imagery that idealized the Virgin Mother, who is unified by the Name of the Other, without any connection with the

reality of the body... [she is] totally within the unsymbolizable thing that resists meaning... she loses herself in the unassertable, below the level of all language. (De Certeau 1992: 34–5)

This then, can serve to summarise what I have been trying to advance concerning the anorexic: the kitchen, the circulation of little substances, the body made of crumbs, cooking but not eating, the body turned into a dishrag (or black hat since everybody has their own style), separation from the Name of the Other, from the body of the Mother, thus bodiless, nameless and impersonal.

But to say that she escapes the symbolic, that she resists meaning and remains 'below the level of all language,' is also to point again to the radicalism of anorexic micro-politics. It is to claim that such a politics is about a double divergence. As Deleuze puts it in a passage, referred to earlier, that explains how enthusiasm relates to this politics:

Anorexics are enthusiasts: they live treason or the double turning-away in several ways. They betray hunger, because hunger tricks them by making them subject to the organism; they betray the family because the family betrays them by subjecting them to the family meal and a whole family politics of consumption; finally, they betray food, because food is treacherous by nature... Trick-the-hunger, trick-the-family, trick-the-food. In short, anorexia is a history of politics: to be the involuted of the organism, the family or the consumer society. There is politics as soon as there is a continuum of intensities (anorexic void and fullness), emission and conquest of food particles (constitution of a body without organs, in opposition to a dietary or organic regime), and above all combination of fluxes (the food flux inters into relation with a clothes flux, a flux of language, a flux of sexuality: a whole, molecular woman-becoming in the anorexic, whether man or woman. Above all, it is not a matter of partial objects. It is true that psychiatry and psychoanalysis do not understand, because they bring everything down to the level of a neuro-organic or symbolic code ('lack, lack...'). (Deleuze 1987: 111)

Never about lack, it is always about rhythm, about the succession, waves and fluxes of voids and fullness.

Danger and Death

In thinking about anorexia I don't intend to recommend it. It is up to everybody to invent their own micro-politics of pain. Anorexia should be understood to represent a particular strategy of resistance, and rescuing it from the inane ideology of an 'eating disorder,' as well as from the blunt theory of a 'consumption' neurosis is a function of such resistance.

Needless to say, the experimentation called anorexia can be dangerous, indeed lethal. The anorexic has to be able to guide the experiment without being guided by it. She has to experiment without ending in the failure of experimentation, the point at which the experiment turns against the experimenter and becomes deadly. The point is to keep the experiment going and thus to keep whoever experiments alive, even if not within the same banal everyday conception of what life is. If the main goal of the micro-politics of masochism or anorexia is to invent the body of waves, the body without organs, then the success of such an experiment means, paradoxically, that the body without organs will never be fully realised, for such a realisation is pure and simple death: a frozen body. The danger of this micro-politics (the same holds for all other such experiments, with drugs, alcohol, food, sleep, but also for molar experiments, for experimentation by definition involves danger) is, as Deleuze puts it, that it can come 'close to going off the rails, to becoming lethal.' That is not a reason to give up on such micro-politics but a call to address the question of the danger that it involves: 'What are the dangers it constantly skirts and the dangers into which it falls?' However, this question should be neither raised nor answered from the perspective of a psychoanalysis capable only of ridiculing the micro-politics of pain with its ready-made answers about the desire to return to the origin and the death drive: 'This is a question that must be taken up by a method other than psychoanalysis: we must try to find out what dangers arise *in the middle of* a real experiment, and not the lack dominating a pre-established interpretation. People are always in the middle of some business, where nothing may be designated as its origin. Always things encountering each other, never things diminishing each other's contribution' (Deleuze 1987: 111).

References

Beckett, Samuel (1958) *Endgame, A Play in One Act*, New York: Grove Press.
Breuer, Josef and Sigmund Freud (1956) *Studies on Hysteria*, London: Hogarth Press.
De Certeau, Michel (1992) *The Mystic Fable*, vol. 1, trans. Michael B. Smith, Chicago: The University of Chicago Press.
De Certeau, Michel, Luce Giard and Pierre Mayol (1998) *The Practice of Everyday Life, Vol. 2: Living & Cooking*, Minneapolis: University of Minnesota Press.
Deleuze, Gilles and Claire Parnet (1987) *Dialogues*, trans. Hugh Tomlinson and Barbara Habberjam, New York: Columbia University Press.
Deleuze, Gilles (1986) *Cinema 1, The Movement-Image*, trans. Hugh Tomlinson and Barbara Habberjam, Minneapolis: University of Minnesota Press.
Deleuze, Gilles (1994) *Difference and Repetition*, trans. Paul Patton, New York: Columbia University Press.

Deleuze, Gilles and Félix Guattari (1992) *A Thausand Plateaus*, trans. Brian Massumi, London: The Athlone Press.

Deleuze, Gilles and Félix Guattari (1994) *What is Philosophy?*, trans. Hugh Tomlinson and Graham Burchell, New York: Columbia University Press.

Derrida, Jacques (1995) ' "Eating Well," or the Calculation of the Subject,' *Points… Interviews, 1974–1994*, trans. Peggy Kamuf et al., Stanford, CA: Stanford University Press.

Emerson, Ralph Waldo (1996) 'Manners,' 'Essays: Second Series,' *Essays & Poems*, New York: The Library of America.

James, William (1992) 'Psychology: Briefer Course,' *Writings 1878–1899*, ed. Gerald E. Myers, New York: The Library of America.

Kafka, Franz (1953) *Letters to Milena*, ed. Willi Haas, trans. Tania and James Stern, New York: Schocken Books.

Kafka, Franz (1976) *Diaries 1910–1923*, ed. Max Brod, trans. Joseph Kresh and Martin Greenberg, New York: Schocken Books.

Woolf, Virginia (1959) *Waves*, New York: Harcourt.

DOI: 10.3366/E1750224108000354

Feminist Lines of Flight from the Majoritarian Subject

Tamsin Lorraine   Swarthmore College

Abstract

This paper characterises Deleuze and Guattari's conception of the majoritarian subject in *A Thousand Plateaus* as a particular – and inevitably transitory – manifestation of sexed and gendered subjectivity emerging with late capitalism from the always mutating flows of creative life and suggests that their notion of the schizo or nomadic subject can inspire feminist solutions to the impasses posed by contemporary forms of sexed, gendered, and sexual identity. Feminism can thus be conceived as a schizoanalytic practice that fosters the kind of alternative subjects for which Deleuze and Guattari call: subjects that move beyond oppressive self–other relations towards a form of subjectivity that can welcome differences as well as the differentiating force of life itself.

Keywords: Deleuze, Guattari, gender, feminism, identity, subjectivity.

Gilles Deleuze and Félix Guattari, in works they wrote separately as well as together, present an ontology of becoming, a conception of the modern subject of late capitalism, and intimations of future forms of humanity with intriguing implications for feminism. Their ontology posits humanity as a flux of always mutating becoming intertwined with creative flows of non-human and inhuman life, and thus contests essentialist views of women and men as well as a binary division between the two. Their conception of the modern 'autonomous' subject posits the latter as inevitably shot through with a multitude of social flows in shifting configurations that can be mapped with respect to specific locations in larger social wholes, and thus suggests a subject produced through collective processes that we can better understand and invites discriminating genealogies of gender in its imbrications with other aspects of social identity. And their notion of the schizo or nomadic subject dramatises possible 'lines of flight' from dominant forms of subjectivity, and thus inspires feminist solutions to the impasses posed by contemporary forms of sexed, gendered, and sexual identity.

In what follows, I characterise Deleuze and Guattari's conception of the modern subject as a particular – and inevitably transitory – manifestation of sexed and gendered subjectivity emerging with late capitalism from the always mutating flows of creative life and I explore the implications of their conception for a feminist project of social change. Although Deleuze and Guattari do not pursue this point the way I will throughout this essay, sexed, gendered, and sexual identity are central features of the oedipal subject, making the question of sexual difference a crucial one, at least if one wants to endorse their project of promoting schizo subjectivity as a project, as I will propose, of moving beyond oppressive self/other relations toward a form of subjectivity that can welcome differences as well as the differentiating force of life itself.

I. Oedipal Subjectivity and the Majoritarian Subject

According to the story Deleuze and Guattari tell in *Anti-Oedipus*, oedipalisation as a psychic structure of human subjectivity arose in the wake of capitalism's deterritorialisation from the social systems of meaning of previous cultures. *Anti-Oedipus* is in large part a critique of psychoanalysis for further entrenching oedipal subjectivity rather than (as Deleuze and Guattari propose) moving us beyond it, but it is important to remember that Deleuze and Guattari 'have never dreamed of saying that psychoanalysis invented Oedipus. Everything points in the opposite direction: the subjects of psychoanalysis arrive already oedipalized, they demand it, they want more' (Deleuze and Guattari 1983: 121). Although they think that psychoanalysis gets the unconscious wrong and has fallen for the ruse oedipal subjectivity entails – that what the subject wants but cannot have is an incestuous relationship with his mother (rather than, as they see it, to engage in forms of desiring production that might unravel or revolutionise the social status quo) – the oedipal subject characterised by psychoanalysis is an ideal type of a fleeting form of modern subjectivity. This type may be actually manifest in a relatively small number of instances given the deterritorialising flows that undermine it as well as the vagaries of family life, but it is a form of subjectivity whose further unravelling they hope to promote. If the oedipal subject is the retrenchment of a more traditional form of subjectivity precipitated by the frantic deterritorialisation of capitalism, the schizo subject is a new form of subjectivity also precipitated by the deterritorialisation of capitalism – and it is the latter subject that Deleuze and Guattari prefer to support.

Although sexed and gendered identity may appear to be primary aspects of personal identity (checking off one's race or religion may or may not be required, but checking off one's sex usually is), on Deleuze and Guattari's view, oedipal subjectivity obscures the multiple social flows implicated in family life. Markers of difference that have stable social significance in the territorial and despotic social formations Deleuze and Guattari describe lose their credibility in a capitalist social formation. Deference to abstract calculations of the market such as the need for workers who can migrate from one workplace to the next in keeping with the skills needed to produce the products that will sell the best take precedence over the significance of concrete relations with others in a variety of relatively stable social networks. Cultural and institutional support for various identities is weakened by the commodification of ethnic and cultural differences. The flows affecting a subject's life are organised around sexed and gendered identities produced through a process of oedipalisation that requires constituting oneself as a lacking subject and taking up a position on either side of a sexual divide. Sexual difference becomes a crucial structural feature in the psychic structure of a personal self who can negotiate the speeds of capitalism without unravelling, but the flows affecting subjects are social, economic, political, cultural, racial, pedagogical, and religious, as much as sexed or gendered (see, for example, Deleuze and Guattari 1983: 274).

While sexual difference is important to the territorial and despotic social formations Deleuze and Guattari describe, it is not personalised in the form of sexed and gendered identity and sexual preference the way it is in modern society.[1] According to Deleuze and Guattari's view, human subjects enter into polyvocal and multiple relations with their world. A child is always making assemblages – pushing an ant along with a stick, jumping in a puddle to see the water splash, blowing bubbles in the milk to see them cascade over the sides. These assemblages unfold not as expressions of the secret desires of a personal self, but through body parts becoming the working parts of assemblages that connect with the world in terms of their capacities to affect and be affected (air plus throat plus milk in glass make bubbles that spill over). Oedipalisation requires the subject to internalise the prohibitions of paternal law: to regain a substitute for the prohibited mother (an incestuous relation with whom, in some sense, comes to represent, according to Deleuze and Guattari, engaging in unregulated desiring production with its immanent satisfactions), one must identify with the father and become an active agent of the law he represents, or become the object desirable enough to obtain passive access to phallic power. This produces a subject whose desire is premised upon lack (one desires what one has lost and cannot have until one lives up to one's ego ideal) rather than upon the creation of connections with the world that unfold creative capacities in living.

Internalisation of paternal law suppresses pursuit of the mutant lines of deterritorialisation that emerge from the swiftly changing circumstances induced by the incessant drive for profit, allowing relative stability of the oedipal subject (if of a paranoid sort) despite the breakdown in traditional codes in living and the habitual patterns of life that actualise such codes. Barred from the creative transformation of productive connection with the world, the oedipal subject of capitalism maintains self-sameness with respect to interchangeable objects of desire through repetition of personalised patterns of meaning and behaviour. Her desiring production is restricted to fantasising the objects that once acquired will give her the satisfaction she seeks. She is thus diverted from engaging in the immanently satisfying production of machines that would connect her in various ways to the flows around her (machines that would extend her capacities and engage her in the kind of on-going metamorphosis that makes subjects hard to pin down). The desire to connect, make things happen, and extend one's capacities and powers to affect and be affected (the productive desire that constitutes active participation in the creative diverging of life) becomes the private desire of a personal self to obtain a substitute for an object of desire prohibited by paternal law (where the latter is understood as the dominant processes regulating social existence in its current configurations).

In *A Thousand Plateaus*, Deleuze and Guattari's characterisation of the modern subject de-emphasises the role of the family in the production of oedipal subjectivity and elaborates the larger social flows that resonate and affirm the constricted desires of a subject premised upon lack. From the moment a child is born, she is immersed in flows of signification and subjectification, and she enacts, through her perceptions, thoughts, actions, and emotions, the habitual patterns and orientations of her location on the social field with its particular configurations of human and non-human flows. The subject emerges from myriad routines and habitual patterns of living in which she understands herself and what she says and does through meanings made available by the practices engaged in at home, at school, at work, at places of worship, at the doctor's office, at court, and so forth, as well as by multiple forms of cultural production ranging from network news and printed materials to video games and cinema. Deleuze and Guattari's notion of the faciality machine suggests that the triangulation of identity with respect to sexual difference in the family is replicated and affirmed with respect to multiple flows of the social field in a way that fixes the subject on a 'white wall' of signification where she can always be categorisable and plunges her into a 'black hole' of subjectification where her psychic habits of self devolve into sterile patterns. Everyone must submit to the dualism machines of subjectification, either identifying their subjective experience with one of two opposing categories in a series of opposing categories or being subjected to such identification by others. A recognisable subject with a specific position vis-à-vis what Deleuze and Guattari call the 'majoritarian subject' is thereby produced 'depending on which faciality trait is retained: male-(female), adult-(child), white-(black, yellow, or red); rational-(animal)' (ATP 292).

The faciality function shows us the form upon which the majoritarian subject is based: 'white, male, adult, "rational," etc., in short, the average European' (Deleuze and Guattari 1987: 292). Faces are produced 'only when the head ceases to be a part of the body, when it ceases to be coded by the body, when it ceases to have a multidimensional, polyvocal corporeal code' (Deleuze and Guattari 1987: 170). Mutant fluxes and flows of the body, for example, various forms of becoming-animal, are no longer elements that are taken up into the socially sanctioned organisation of human individuals. 'Bodies are disciplined, corporeality dismantled, becomings-animal hounded out' (Deleuze and Guattari 1987: 181). The complexity of embodied existence is reduced to what can be captured and coded through the faces that are socially recognisable (faces that show up on society's white wall as readable) and psychically convincing (faces that can be internalised as one's personal identity). Faces thus entail a reduction of one's lived experience of another human being in all her specificity to the selected perception of another in terms of relatively fixed social categories of identity. They also entail a personal psychic identity that comes to, in a sense, stand in for the unrepresentable subtlety, variation, and ambiguity in the lived experience of one's own corporeality.

Sexed and gendered identities are crucial to the stabilising identifications required by the faciality machines; taking up a definitive stance with respect to a transcendent representation of desire separated from the differentiating flux of life – the phallus as signifier of whatever one might desire (with its implications of the passive or active relation of the sexed subject vis-à-vis the likelihood of achieving satisfaction) – renders the lines of becoming connecting one to the world imperceptible and thus totalises a self that can be ranked with respect to the majoritarian subject. Forming a central identity as a woman or a man with a specific gender identity thus entails a conception of self in relative autonomy from the world who takes a passive or active desiring stance with respect to that world. This division of humanity into two sexually differentiated groups obscures a wide range of social investments of the contemporary social field stratified into various configurations of power by highlighting sexed identity as key to determining who one is and how to live one's life. A variegated range of differences among human subjects is thus reduced in significance when compared to identification with one of two categories, woman or man. This binary configuration allows resonating patterns of binary identifications that situate subjects with respect to the majoritarian subject in ways that clearly delineate one's position according to a relatively static social hierarchy.

At the level of the lived orientation of embodied subjectivity, each subject, whether oedipalised or not, lives out her life as a unique configuration of the concrete flows of physiological, corporeal, and semiotic processes that inform her day-to-day life. How well this orientation fits with the categories through which she is designated and interpellated by the various practices she engages depends upon her specific situation. No subject in contemporary society can escape dealing with sex and gender categories in one form or another. Whether one lives out these designations and interpellations in comfortable conformity or painful dissonance depends upon whether the multiple forces converging in the durations one lives resonate with dominant memory (that is, the representational memories and history sanctioned by the mainstream) or induce varying tendencies toward counter-memories and minoritarian resistance. Furthermore, binary sexual difference turns out to entail a form of subjectivity structured in terms of bifurcating categories that valorise some subjects by marginalising others. Identification with one or the other of two sexually differentiated positions (despite the molecular connections subverting or complicating that identification) is paradigmatic for other selections made from the faces of the faciality machines. The active/passive dichotomies of sexual difference are replicated in other social binaries with one identification of two possibilities being always better or worse (that is, either closer to or further from the majoritarian subject).

If a variegated range of social flows (from physiological and cultural flows related to one's able-bodiedness and race to economic and political flows related to one's class and political affiliation) become subsumed under one's sexed and gendered identity with respect to a familial story about sexual difference (one is a disabled woman or black woman rather than a disabled or black human being; one is disabled *or* abled, black *or* white, just as one is a woman *or* a man), then the latter will loom large in one's attempts to live a meaningful life. Troubling the waters of binary sexed and gendered identities by revealing the complexities subverting them as well as their imbrications with other aspects of identity would thus appear to be especially threatening to forms of subjectivity organised with respect to the majoritarian subject. If this is the case, the feminist imperative to map sex and gender in relation to other social designations could be said to be a project of mapping forms of subjectivity structured in terms of their divergence from a normative subject in order to explore and experiment with the possibilities implicit in our present of a subjectivity that could welcome differences without ranking them. Mapping subjectivity in terms of sex and gender from this perspective respects the importance they play in orienting lived experience in its contemporary formations at the same time as it fosters lines of flight that could lead to forms of subjectivity that do not require marginalising others.

II. Lived Orientations and Feminist Genealogies

Linda Alcoff, in an insightful essay on identity, argues that we need to conceive identity as more than a category. Identity entails an interpretative horizon that 'should be understood not simply as a set of beliefs but as a complex (meaning internally heterogeneous) set of presuppositions and perceptual orientations, some of which are manifest as a kind of tacit presence in the body' (Alcoff 2006: 113). She cites George Lakoff and Mark Johnson's work demonstrating that the concepts we use in everyday life emerge from 'largely unconscious embodied conceptual systems' (Alcoff 2006: 113). And she draws from the phenomenological descriptions of Maurice Merleau-Ponty, Simone de Beauvoir, Sandra Bartky, and Iris Young to indicate how a lived orientation of the body in the world constitutes a kind of implicit knowledge. On Alcoff's account, identity is an orientation to the world lived in the gestures, movements, and actions of the body at a non-conscious level as well as in the presuppositions, assumptions, and beliefs of a linguistic orientation. Both together comprise an interpretative horizon that grounds a subject in a perspective that is lived as her own. Social identity is not simply the categories into which one fits, but an interpretative horizon shared with certain others that affects what and how one perceives. These identities are experienced in terms of the imbrications of social flows that converge in the various assemblages through which day-to-day life is lived rather than the abstract categories of identity to which people are often reduced. Identity is thus not necessarily something that is inflicted upon one by others; it is an orientation experienced as one's own that emerges through participation in collective patterns of corporeal and symbolic activity. This is why claiming an identity through a rewriting of dominant history can be so important. In articulating and asserting such an identity, a perspective grounded in patterns of collective living experienced by a minoritarian group is brought into conscious awareness and made the basis for an alternative epistemological claim to that of the dominant culture about the nature of social reality. 'Real' identity is thus, according to Alcoff, experienced as an orientation grounded in often non-conscious patterns of body, mind, and speech so habitual that they can appear (if they appear at all) to be inevitable or natural.

What Alcoff calls 'real' identity is, from Deleuze and Guattari's perspective, the perceptual, cognitive, affective, and embodied orientations of a subject sustained through the habitual patterns of physiological, social, and cultural processes that constitute one as an embodied human subject. Orientations constituted and sustained through organic processes experienced in imbrication with the semiotic and corporeal signifying and subjectifying processes of human living inform how one experiences the world. If one's corporeal and/or psychic anomalies are such that one cannot take up positions with which one can identify without dissonance, then one will experience a sense of discomfort, a sense of not being at home in the world.[2] This discomfort will deepen if dissonance results in derogatory descriptions or exclusion. Subjects marked in terms of their divergence from the majoritarian norm are designated as somehow less entitled to other forms of social power. Unless one can find alternatives, practices available to others as an extension of their capacities into action in the world (of a more or less powerful sort) will block one's lines of becoming and decrease one's power. Individual and collective orientations suffer damaging marginalisation and uncomfortable dissonance when they are subjected to faciality machines in ways that mark their divergence from the majoritarian norm and block potential capacities for affecting and being affected from unfolding.

When the lived orientations Alcoff describes as 'real' identity are extended and elaborated in the minoritarian form of, for example, a feminist gender identity or an antiracist raced identity, identity becomes a form of self-naming that extends some of the lines of flight always insisting in any subject in its divergence from the majoritarian subject.

The faciality machines that designate either/or identity positions through prevalent ways of speaking and patterns of activity that resonate with the majoritarian subject attempt to cancel out the corporeal and conceptual fluxes that would lead human subjects in their becoming to resist the dominant patterns of signification and subjectification: you are a man *or* a woman, you are black *or* white. Resistant identities are identities in process – they create new identities rooted in fluxes of living that continually vary from the dominant norm, refusing to let those variations be assimilated to binary categories or their implicit tendencies blocked from unfolding new ways of living.

Subjecting a range of evidence to abstract social categories like race and gender tends to obscure the imbrications of social flows as well as the 'intensities' (implicit tendencies that could unfold in new ways of being) insisting in them. Understanding identity categories such as those designating one's gender, race, (dis)ability, or sexuality in terms of the concrete situations in which they are used reveals the varying flows that converge in the pragmatic contexts in which embodied subjects are submitted to and/or identify with specific categories. Mapping these flows with respect to one another allows one to see how various flows of meaning produce identity categories inflected by the specific forms social flows take in a given time and place. For example, Abby Wilkerson's mapping of erotophobia, in an essay using disability and queer perspectives to explore continuities in the effect of erotophobia on oppressed groups, shows how social flows can be coded in divergent and yet mutually reinforcing ways. Wilkerson argues that a paraplegic may be coded as asexual, an African American as hypersexual, and a lesbian as perverted, but in all cases, the effect is to render the lived experience of one's sexuality less comfortable, thus blocking one's power in the world to a greater or lesser extent. She presents some examples of how erotophobic judgements of the sexual behaviours or 'natures' of members of various groups suggests that

> [c]ultural erotophobia is not merely a general taboo against open discussions of sexuality, and displays of sexual behaviour, but a very effective means of creating and maintaining social hierarchies, not only those of sexuality but those of gender, race, class, age, and physical and mental ability. (Wilkerson 2002: 41)

Medical literature that presents moralising restrictions on the sexuality of the physically or cognitively disabled, hypersexualised images of African American and Latino men, legal obstacles to the sexual agency of lesbian, gay, bisexual, and transgender people, the shame and alienation connected to the sexuality of heterosexual women that Sandra Bartky discusses in her book, *Femininity and Domination* (Wilkerson 2002: 42–5): these are some of the effects of social practices that designate certain bodies as deviant. From Deleuze and Guattari's perspective we can say that it is through such practices that bodies and their desires are delineated in terms of their distance from the majoritarian subject acting as an orienting reference point (in more or less overt forms) in those practices. Such delineation, through more or less subtle approbation (a doctor who refuses to discuss birth control with a disabled patient) or outright exclusion (laws against sodomy) renders certain lines of becoming uncomfortable, dissonant, or impossible, diminishing the power of those groups and their individual members to affect and be affected in the process.

Feminists inspired by the Foucauldian notion of genealogy have mapped various aspects of the social field to investigate how identity designations have evolved over time, leaving legacies in the present that might not be immediately obvious. If we look at some feminist genealogies of race, for example, we discover not only a telling resonance with Deleuze and Guattari's notions of faciality and the majoritarian subject, but how designations of the Eurocentric faciality machines are implicated with capitalist and colonialist investments of the social field, and how sex and gender designations intertwine with race designations according to the configurations of forces of specific times and places (see, for example, Lawrence 2003, McWhorter 2004, and Warnke 2005). Other feminist genealogies show that sex and gender are not only intertwined with race, but with other perhaps less obvious (at least if you are closer to the majoritarian norm) designations of cognitive and physical ability. For example, Anna Stubblefield argues that the concept of feeblemindedness became linked with ' "off-white" ethnicity, poverty, and gendered conceptions of a lack of moral character' (Stubblefield 2007: 162) in the eugenics movement of the first three decades of the twentieth century in the US. The eugenics movement was widespread and according to Stubblefield its impact still influences scientific research and public policy. In her investigation of how, in particular, 'feeble-minded' white women became subject to coercive sterilisation, Stubblefield examines distinctions white elites drew between the white race and other races; (untainted) whites (supposedly) have the intellectual capacity to produce 'civilisation':

> the development of agriculture, science and technology (in forms that white elites recognize); sophisticated (according to white perception) cultural

products such as literature, music, and art; and the development of complex (according to white perception) societal organization and forms of government. (Stubblefield 2007: 169)

Stubblefield cites research by scientists such as Paul Broca, Robert Chambers, and J. Langdon Down, in the mid-nineteenth century that investigated how to measure intelligence by first assuming that white people were more intelligent than black people, and then, on the basis of that assumption, construing differences between white and black people as reasons for why white people were further along an evolutionary path of ethnic types than black people. When Henry Hubert Goddard, writing in the early twentieth century, described intelligence (understood in terms of this model of ethnic evolution) as hereditary and impervious to environmental influence, the stage was set for designating 'heritable' forms of white impurity (Stubblefield 2007: 172).

In 1908, Goddard adapted Alfred Binet's intelligence test for use in the United States by adding the category of 'moron' (designating people with a mental age of eight to twelve) to the original scale that included the 'idiot' (designating people with a mental age of two or younger) and 'imbecile' (designating people with a mental age of three to seven years). The notion that extreme poverty was hereditary and linked to the moral defect 'of a supposedly shameless willingness to live on public charity' (Stubblefield 2007: 173) was a widespread belief that became increasingly linked to the concept of the moron in family studies done in the early twentieth century. Feeblemindedness became linked with 'white poverty, off-whiteness, and lack of civilization-building skills' and the 'category of the moron – the feebleminded person who appears normal but who is prone to immorality, incapable of being a contributing citizen in a democratic society, and who will pass feeblemindedness on to his or her offspring' became 'a powerful device for drawing a distinction between tainted and pure white people' (Stubblefield 2007: 176). In addition, white women who demonstrated their failure to understand their role in the advancement of civilisation by engaging in unchaste behaviour manifested, like impoverished white women and off-white women, a 'lack' of intellect that tainted their whiteness. Thus, intertwined constructions of race, class, gender, and cognitive dis/ability came together in a conception of feeblemindedness that 'became gendered in a way that led to women bearing the brunt of eugenic sterilization' (Stubblefield 2007: 178–9).

'Disabled' subjects may be divergent enough from the majoritarian norm that their disability becomes a salient feature of their designated identity. Even in such cases, however, their sexed and gendered identity will be central to how that identity is interpreted and lived. Stubblefield's mapping reveals specific physiological, economic, colonising, and cultural flows in the use of the term 'feeble-minded' that manifest the imbrications of gender, race, cognitive (dis)ability, and economic status in that designation in a way that belies the primacy given to sex and gender in organising and understanding the converging flows of concrete individuals. A wide range of practices resonate with familial positioning in order to reinforce and naturalise distance from the majoritarian subject. Maps like Wilkerson's reveal the social investments and configurations of power that such positioning conceals.

In addition to revealing the multiple forces that come together in one designation of social identity, feminist maps reveal critical points in the present where intensification of various sorts could result in significant change. Thus, Wilkerson and Stubblefield's genealogies reveal relations of flows of which we may not have been aware that condition our understanding of disability. Intensifying these connections in new ways of understanding designations of disability and racial designations, as well as the social practices related to them, could in turn lead to action from within the relevant practices that shift them (to a larger or lesser extent) into divergent forms of those practices or directly challenge them (through discursive critique or some other form of resistance). These genealogies, incomplete as they are, show how important it is to understand how identity designations – be they those of sex, gender, sexuality, race or otherwise – emerge and are interpreted in keeping with specific investments of the social field best understood in terms of the confluence of multiple forces of particular durations. The bifurcating sorting of personal identity into yes/no categories obscures the shifting vagaries of their evolution as they are put into effect in a multitude of day-to-day situations. Although an emphasis on the personal identity of an autonomous subject and the demand for clearly defined identity designations tend to suggest that a given identity is a property of persons, on Deleuze and Guattari's view, identity is produced, reproduced, sustained, and transformed through the unfolding of social life over specific periods of time in particular places.

A designation of gender, race, or disability can never, from Deleuze and Guattari's perspective, be a static category. Its meanings inevitably shift along with the faciality machines (as they are actualised in specific patterns of meaning and activity) that enact it as well as the molecular flows of lived orientations and identifications that resist those machines. Such shifts are in response to the convergent forces affecting the relevant assemblages and will resonate with patterns organised around the majoritarian subject or proliferate lines of flight. Words such as 'disabled' or 'feeble-minded' and the racial, gendered, and economic connotations associated with them, leave traces in the present of which we may be unaware, even if those specific words are no longer used. Ways of speaking and doing become habitual patterns that self-replicate even if in doing so they continually diverge from past repetitions. Mapping an association among variations in cognitive style, skin colour, financial income, and cultural practices of the duration connecting us to an earlier time renders some of the relations now only implicit explicit, making us more aware of the habitual patterns informing our naturalised reality, and thus provide insight into how to shift those patterns in ways we can support.

These genealogies track social practices that constitute subject positions informing the categories through which people are designated as well as identify themselves. These practices, from Deleuze and Guattari's perspective, are corporeal and semiotic assemblages that tend to replicate and extend themselves, thus settling into stratified configurations of power. Individual human beings with their personal identities and desires emerge as individual solutions to the problem of subjectivity from processes they collectively share in various ways with others. Although sexed and gendered identity is a crucial feature of dominant forms of subjectivity, these genealogies show how other investments of the social field are equally, if not more, crucial. Even when one's personal identity is still experienced in terms of one's sex, gender, and sexuality (for example, one's primary identification is as a woman), these genealogies show the myriad social investments that coalesce around that identity (it turns out a woman who primarily identifies as a woman may be more likely to be relatively closer to the majoritarian norm and so has not been confronted with other ways that she differs from that norm – that is, she is a physically and cognitively 'normal,' white, heterosexual, middle-class woman).

From Deleuze and Guattari's perspective, modern subjectivity, insofar as it is oriented with respect to the majoritarian subject, thus entails organising multiple flows and investments of the social field in terms of sexual difference. This structuring plays out through the oedipalising function of the family and the faciality machines that confirm and elaborate the binary structure of oedipalisation. Oedipalisation and the faciality machines that produce the personal identity of modern subjectivity thus operate not only to render the continuous variation in human becoming that might extend into new forms of subjectivity non-productive, but also to turn collective stories about power investments into personal stories about achieving meaningful lives. Although Deleuze and Guattari do not themselves pursue this point, this makes feminism an intervention that targets sex, gender, and sexuality as a crucial fault line in modern forms of subjectivity that is just the starting point for unravelling multiple configurations of power detrimental to our collective unfolding.

III. Nomadic Subjectivity and Feminist Change

The deterritorialising of cultural codes precipitated by capitalism opens human existence to an unprecedented amount of creative evolution by releasing old constraints upon proliferating change. Thus, capitalism actually enacts more of the differing and diverging becoming of life and so, according to Deleuze and Guattari, on the one hand, puts us in a better situation to become more aware of life as process, but on the other hand, has produced a reterritorialisation onto oedipal or majoritarian subjectivity, the reduction of productive desire to desire premised on lack, and the incessant pressure to produce and consume. The former tendency they align with their notion of schizophrenia and a nomadic subject able to creatively evolve and the latter tendencies they associate with paranoia and absolute systems of belief where all meaning is, as Eugene Holland helpfully puts it, 'permanently fixed and exhaustively defined by a supreme authority, figure-head, or god' (Holland 1999: 3). Thus, along with the high speeds of contemporary life with its frantic pace of technological change and globalisation goes paranoid reterritorialisation onto consumerism as well as fundamentalist religion and fascist politics. Faciality machines are not universal to human life; subjectivity in modern capitalism requires excluding more of the corporeal fluxes running through any line of human becoming than the other two social formations Deleuze and Guattari describe (although this, in itself, does not guarantee the kind of desiring production Deleuze and Guattari would like to promote). Rather than explore possible connections among micropercepts and affects that could lead to aggregates of perception and feeling that violate current opinion and consensus representations of reality, faciality machines interpret sensation as the meaningful experience of a recognisable subject. Rather than pursue the physiological, social, and cultural permutations that inevitably result from hybrid forces converging in particular locations, faciality machines interpret anomalies as exceptions that do not affect the norm or as exceptions that require new categories that resonate with the system as a whole. This entails cancelling out subtleties in individual and collective experience and blocking exploration of alternative connections.

Facialisation entails an embodied orientation organised in terms of a personal identity. That is, all desires of the body are of *one* body with a psychic self that is (more or less) unified with a coherent history that can be represented and collated with the narratives of other members of the community. Sexed and gendered identity forms an important fault line of this self since it is through familial positioning with respect to sexual difference that the multiplicity of social flows affecting subjectivity are totalised in a self that is assimilable to the faciality machines of capitalism. Personal identity, especially as it is regulated by the faciality machines that percolate throughout the semiotic and corporeal practices that insist on clearly delineated subjects with identities that fit into already laid out parameters (to register for public school, I need to designate age, sex, and residence; to walk into a restroom I need to know to which sex my body conforms), becomes the organising reference point for lived experience. If a lived experience cannot be referred to such reference points, it may be unrepresentable and excluded from having an impact (the knowledge I gain independently of a recognised school may not gain me entry to the conference I want to attend), or it can render lived experience either dissonant or unlivable (ambiguous sexed or gendered identity can make life painfully confusing). But on Deleuze and Guattari's view, personal identity is not necessary for non-psychotic subjectivity. Habitual refrains and some sort of constriction on desiring production are necessary for relatively stable forms of human subjects to be sustainable. But subjectivity is a self-organising system of becoming with relative autonomy from surrounding flows grounded in a wide range of territorialised processes that allow emotions, perceptions, and day-to-day life to stabilise into habitual patterns. In a social formation premised upon a lacking subject threatened with a loss of humanity insofar as she or he breaks the rules (where the majoritarian subject is the norm for what it is to be human and any deviation from that norm is carefully observed and marked), unregulated refrains in living are not allowed extension into new patterns. Productive desire must be reduced to the lacking desire of a self still waiting to be completed (the child's desire to swirl water into dirt to make mud must give way to the desire *to be* a chef or a scientist rather than simply to make connections), and identity must be computed from the bifurcating patterns of social recognition that select constants from a wide range of continuous variation in order to plug those constants into already delineated rules of living (a woman who is disabled must no longer be interested in sex since she no longer fits the subject positions designated in countless narratives and scenarios emerging in multiple social practices about 'what happens when one is sexual,' a mother who does not feel the kind of 'maternal' love for all her children depicted in various forms of cultural production as well as assumed in social practices connected to childcare, pedagogy, and citizenship must be an inhuman monster).

From a psychoanalytic perspective, immersion in a world of partial objects where corporeal fluxes connect (or do not connect) in immanently unfolding flows with surrounding flows where neither self or other, subject or object, are points of reference is a psychotic nightmare. Deleuze and Guattari present us with the provocative possibility that desire does not have to be about what a personal self wants, but could be about connecting with the world, making things happen, and experiencing what happens in ways that defy subject/object and self/other dichotomies. Self/other dichotomies obscure the physiological, social, and cultural flows I share with others; I live at the same speed as other organisms with similar configurations of processes (as I discover in the assemblages I make with others) and the semiotic and material assemblages that condition my individual speech and actions are often the same. On Deleuze and Guattari's view, a personal self or identity as a totalised point of origin to which to refer all desire operates as a kind of stranglehold on the individual and the capacities it could unfold as well as the assemblages into which it could enter. By referring my desires to a sexed self with a gender and a sexuality computed according to the faciality machines, I block off intensification of other tendencies insisting in me – tendencies concerning sense experience and perception as well as emotions and beliefs – that could be extended into new ways of living my subjectivity and new ways of connecting with my world including the other subjects within it.

The famous case of John/Joan (who I will henceforth call by his real name when living as the sex he ultimately chose, David) is a sad example of how difficult it can be to live one's humanity in a social formation that demands a recognisable identity sorted through the faciality machines.[3] When a botched circumcision led to an anomaly in organic sex (David's penis was damaged beyond repair), a choice was made to try and repress the anomalous range of continuous variation in human organisms he manifested by surgically altering him, designating him as female, and concealing from him his initial status as male. Judith Butler's rendition of his story brings out the violence to which the people trying to deal with his situation subjected him. Although as he grew older he refused to comply, he was submitted to practices designed to remake him organically so that he would fit certain categories (surgery and hormone therapy), as well as subjectively so that he would identify in particular ways (socialisation that encouraged him to engage in 'feminine' behaviour such as cooking and playing with dolls and interviews that encouraged him to have 'feminine' desires).[4]

From Deleuze and Guattari's perspective, there was no true self attached to either David's 'real' sex (his clearly male body as it existed before the accident) or his gender identity as it had been promoted through subjectification procedures designed to create a female gender identity (being identified and treated as a girl, being subjected to interviews designed to elicit 'female' desires and so forth). David's flow of individuation involved a convergence of physiological, semiotic, and subjectifying forces to which he – as a self-organising process of subjectivity needing to navigate the practices of his social location – had to respond in order to solve the problem of living a life. Although David did achieve his desire to marry and have a family, his life was, by all accounts, difficult, and he committed suicide at the age of 38. It is impossible to know why he made the choice to end his life, but one can imagine how painful dissonance between one's lived experience in all the molecular complexity of one's lived orientation and the molar subject positions designating one's identity in a way that demands the erasure of such complexity can become. His situation was anomalous in a way that could not be easily cancelled out; he simply was neither male nor female in the same way as his peers, given physiological anomalies as well as anomalies in his socialisation.

Susan Stryker, a male-to-female transsexual who refuses assimilating explanations of her actions (such as the explanation that she was 'really' a woman who simply needed to change her body to fit her true identity), is a happier example of how anomalous gender identity can play out in that she is able to intensify and extend her capacities to affect and be affected by the world in ways that challenge the binaries of the faciality machines. She speaks out publicly about her situation and she is a respected member of a transgender community that challenges binary designations of sexed and gendered identity. She thus defies erasure of the range of continuous variation manifest in her particular actualisation of humanity despite her deviance from the norm. She gives a provocative challenge to those who would denounce her and her choices (in a performance piece presented in, as she puts it, 'genderfuck drag' at an interdisciplinary, academic conference)[5]:

> I find no shame... in acknowledging my egalitarian relationship with non-human material Being; everything emerges from the same matrix of possibilities.... [T]he Nature you bedevil me with is a lie. Do not trust it to protect you from what I represent, for it is a fabrication that cloaks

the groundlessness of the privilege you seek to maintain for yourself at my expense. You are as constructed as me; the same anarchic Womb has birthed us both. (Stryker 1999)

David and Stryker both, in different ways, resist the faciality machines that would recuperate their inassimilable differences to binary categories of designation and interpellation. If David had difficulties in identifying with the categories assigned him (when he was forced to identify as a girl despite his lived dissonance with that designation) as well as the categories he finally chose (by choosing to identify as male upon discovering some of what had been hidden from him about the story of his life), it was not because he wanted to challenge traditional notions of sex and gender. What he wanted was to live a meaningful life. What his story shows, perhaps, is how important a sense of self that coheres with one's lived orientations is to making one's life meaningful and therefore livable. We want to connect with the world, affect and be affected, in ways that resonate with a self-understanding and life narrative that makes sense to us, whether or not that sense of self is conventional or dissonant. In Deleuze and Guattari's terms, we might say that subjects need to extend not only their embodied capacities to make things happen, but also their psychic, cognitive, and emotional capacities to make sense of how they fit into larger wholes. David's lived experience was too dissonant for a number of reasons (anatomical, hormonal, cultural, familial) to easily fit into social patterns of making sense – ways of speaking, interpreting, and behaving available to him through collective practices of the social field dictating intelligible behaviour and interpretations – making it difficult for him to feel worthy as a human being.

Deleuze and Guattari's characterisation of subjectivity posits a subject who emerges from collective physiological and social processes as an individual process in its own right by sustaining habitual patterns distinguishing it as an individual from other processes around it. As a specific formation of physiological, social, and linguistic matter with actualised capacities – replete with hidden potential and tendencies structured by virtualities that are part of the wider non-human as well as human field conditioning its becoming – the subject is able to affect as well as be affected by what is around it. But its separation is always provisional, its form always on the verge of differentiating into something else, and the actualisation of its capacities always dependent upon the actualities and intensities that it is and with which it comes into contact.

Nomadic subjects emerge from collective patterns of living with the configuration of social and non-human forces unique to the becoming of specific processes of individuation. The individuation of such subjects cannot be represented. It emerges as a lived orientation constituting one's perceptions, thoughts, emotions, and perspectives through the territorialisations of unique individuations and communities grounded in the material reality of shared patterns of living. Some orientation with respect to the identity designations of mainstream social practices is necessary for subjectivity. One's 'personal' identity can be thought in terms of the 'molar' designations of the faciality machines that enable negotiation of dominant social systems of meaning or in terms of lived orientations too subtle to be captured through such designations, but which one could choose to assert by naming them. Heightened awareness of converging flows and the habitual patterns that orient one along with a sense of one's own location and places to intervene in order to affect individual and collective forms of self-production could allow resolution of the dissonance often arising between the two forms of identity as well as enable collective compositions that enhance mutually joyful becoming. Nomadic subjectivity as an alternative to oedipal subjectivity invites us to engage in a dynamic process of self-naming rather than reduce ourselves to static self-representations. Identity designations are representations that do not capture the nuances of lived orientations and can block lines of flight by putting people in opposition with one another despite the orientations they share. Drifting from the identity designations of faciality machines in order to experiment with joyful connections entails relinquishing some of the control derived through representational intelligence with its penchant for categorisation in order to trust the affective guidance of intuitive insight into processes of becoming. Becoming more aware of how one's subjectivity is produced allows one to participate more actively in one's self-production, develop skilful ways to synchronise becoming with others, and deterritorialise from identity designations in order to unfold new solutions to the problems life poses. Flexible living entails individual deterritorialisation from personal identity as well as collective deterritorialisations from majoritarian subjectivity. A politics influenced by Deleuze and Guattari would investigate different durations, the mutually reinforcing reference points of the faciality machines among those durations, and the places where intensification of virtual tendencies might unfold new answers to how to live together.

Deleuze and Guattari's conception of human subjectivity emphasises its continuity with the inhuman force of creative life. This emphasis fosters working with rather than against the differentiating forces of life of which we are a part. This ontology conceives individual human beings as singular individuals who more or less diverge from the flows of life currently sustaining themselves in the recognisably human forms with which we are familiar. The question of one's humanity thus shifts from that of measuring up to an essential form of humanity (with respect to which many are found wanting) to the question of what diverging flows of humanity we want to foster in the inevitably diverging and differentiating flux of human life. Shifting the question in this way has practical impact on identity questions key to feminist thought. Women, as well as others who are 'other' to the paradigmatic subject of contemporary culture, have been denigrated for somehow failing to measure up to an ideal norm of what it means to be human. But such a norm assumes an ontology where the form one's humanity takes may well count as a deviation. One strategy of feminism, understandably enough, has been to contest what that essence is in order to make room for women. Shifting to an ontology of becoming suggests a different kind of strategy. If what it means to be human is not fixed, if human becoming entails creative evolution – if what it means to be human consists in the specific forms humanity actually takes and could unfold rather than a human essence that is then instantiated more or less well – then what feminists need to do is map where we are in order to find the best places to intervene and foster the human forms we would most like to support. The question then becomes not who we have always been and always will be, but how to make the mechanisms that create subjects and identities better function in keeping with our own becomings.

Feminism could be seen as an untimely schizo practice designed to intervene with contemporary configurations of modern subjectivity that involve suppression and oppression of subjects that deviate from a majoritarian norm with the fault lines of sexed, gendered, and sexual identity as its starting point. Deleuze and Guattari provide a narrative about the formation and production of those subjects that suggest critical points of intervention that could move us beyond binary categorisation of sex and gender and the oppression it entails. By distinguishing subjectivity as patterns of lived activity from faciality machines that designate identity they give us a way of understanding how we could be subjects without the binary designations that we currently think of as crucial to being any kind of subject at all. But they do not think we can simply choose to leave those binary machines behind. Rather, they recommend carefully mapping where we are in order to find vitalising paths that extend the tendencies resisting binary designations. And they suggest that rather than be paranoid about the anarchic chaos we imagine moving beyond such binaries could cause, that we consider the capacities we could unfold if we could open up to the impersonal and inhuman flows around us. They present us with alternative conceptions of subjectivity as relatively stabilised patterns of physiological, corporeal, and semiotic activity that mutate over time in keeping with the flows that constitute them and the flows with which they come into contact, but which, as self-organising systems, and, in particular, human self-organising systems with the capacity to intuit the durational whole, can consciously participate in their creative evolution. And while such participation does not entail the masterful control of the autonomous subject as conceived by traditional modernity, it does entail ways of being more skilful than others in coming into joyful synchrony with the flows around it. Feminism, as a theoretical and pragmatic process, can intuit ways of living our sex and gender that are more affirming of the continuous range of variation in being sexed and gendered becoming-human entails. By mapping where we are and finding lines of flight from majoritarian subjectivity that can extend our capacities in ways that synchronise with others, feminists, along with other forms of minoritarian and schizo becoming, can promote a joyfully collective and open-ended process of becoming-human.

References

Ahmed, Sara (2006) 'Orientations: Toward a Queer Phenomenology', *GLQ* 12:4.

Alcoff, Linda M. (2006) 'Real Identities', in L. M. Alcoff, *Visible Identities: Race, Gender, and the Self*, New York: Oxford University Press, pp. 84–129.

Bartky, Sandra Lee (1990) *Femininity and Domination: Studies in the Phenomenology of Oppression*, New York: Routledge.

Butler, Judith (2004) 'Doing Justice to Someone: Sex Reassignment and Allegories of Transsexuality', in J. Butler, *Undoing Gender*, New York: Routledge, pp. 57–74.

Colapinto, John (1997) 'The True Story of John/Joan', *The Rolling Stone*, pp. 54–97.

Colapinto, John (2000) *As Nature Made Him: The Boy Who Was Raised as a Girl*, New York: HarperCollins.

Colapinto, John (2004) 'Gender Gap: What Were the Real Reasons Behind David Reimer's Suicide?' *Slate*. Online at http://www.slate.com/id/2101678/.

Deleuze, Gilles and Félix Guattari (1983) *Anti-Oedipus: Capitalism and Schizophrenia*, trans. Robert Hurley, Mark Seem, and Helen R. Lane, Minneapolis: University of Minnesota Press.

Deleuze, Gilles and Félix Guattari (1987) *A Thousand Plateaus: Capitalism and Schizophrenia*, trans. Brian Massumi, Minneapolis: University of Minnesota Press.

Diamond, Milton (1997) 'Sexual Identity and Sexual Orientation in Children with Traumatized or Ambiguous Genitalia', *The Journal of Sex Research*, 34:2, pp. 199–211.

Diamond, Milton and Sigmundsen, Keith (1997) 'Sex Reassignment at Birth: A Long-Term Review and Clinical Implications', *Archives of Pediatrics and Adolescent Medicine* 151 (3), pp. 298–304.

Foucault, Michel (1978) *The History of Sexuality: Vol. I: An Introduction*, New York: Vintage Books.

Holland, Eugene W. (1999) *Deleuze and Guattari's Anti-Oedipus*, New York: Routledge.

Lawrence,Bonita (2003) 'Gender, Race, and the Regulation of Native Identity in Canada and the United States: An Overview', *Hypatia* 18:2, pp. 3–31.

McWhorter, Ladelle (2004) 'Sex, Race, and Biopower: A Foucauldian Genealogy', *Hypatia*, 19:3, pp. 38–62.

Money, John and Green, Richard (1969) *Transsexualism and Sex Reassignment*, Baltimore: Johns Hopkins University Press.

Nietzsche, Friedrich (1989) *On the Genealogy of Morals*, New York: Vintage Books.

Stryker, Susan (1999) 'My Words to Victor Frankenstein Above the Village of Chamounix - Performing Transgender Rage'. Online at Transsexual Women's Resources, http://www.annelawrence.com/twr/mywords.html. Originally printed in *GLQ*, 1:3, pp. 237–54.

Stubblefield, Anna (2007) ' "Beyond the Pale": Tainted Whiteness, Cognitive Disability, and Eugenic Sterilization', *Hypatia*, 22:2, pp. 162–81.

Warnke, Georgia (2005) 'Race, Gender, and Antiessentialist Politics', *Signs*, 31:1, pp. 93–116.

Wilkerson, Abby (2002) 'Disability, Sex Radicalism, and Political Agency', *NWSA Journal*, 14:3, pp. 33–57.

Notes

1. Deleuze and Guattari's account is compatible with Foucault's reading of sexed identity as taking on new importance in the circulation of biopower and the management of large groups of people emerging in the eighteenth century. Whereas one's sex in premodern times had significance in the role one would play and the patterns of social living in which one participated, it was not key to personal identity, on both these accounts, until the emergence of a modern subject with its increasingly interiorised psychic structure (see Foucault 1978). See Nietzsche's *Genealogy of Morals* for an account of the interiorisation of subjectivity in the context of Christianity that influences Deleuze and Guattari's account (Nietzsche 1989).

2. Sara Ahmed presents an example of an evocative phenomenological account of how a queer orientation can precipitate such dissonance (Ahmed 2006).

3. 'John/Joan' was actually David Reimer. For more information on this case from various perspectives, see Colapinto 1997, 2000, and 2004, Diamond 1997, Diamond and Sigmundsen 1997, and Money 1997. I am particularly indebted to Judith Butler's provocative rendition of this case that brings out the problem David posed to the people who responded to him by attempting to render him intelligible from competing perspectives as a problem of a humanity that exceeds intelligibility. On Butler's view: 'it is precisely the ways in which he is not fully recognizable, fully disposable, fully categorizable, that his humanness emerges' (Butler 2004: 73).

4. David's situation was particularly contentious since there were at least two views of who he 'really' was that were being promoted and contested. To oversimplify what were more complicated and evolving positions over the course of a long

debate, John Money, a medical psychologist and founder of the Gender Identity Institute at Johns Hopkins University, thought gender identity was malleable and hoped David's case would prove him right (it helped that David had an identical twin – the perfect complement to an experiment in manipulating gender identity through socialisation) and Milton Diamond, a sex researcher involved in a long-standing battle with Money, believed gender identity had a hormonal basis. See Diamond 1997, Diamond and Sigmundsen 1997, and Money 1997.

5. Stryker describes her outfit as 'combat boots, threadbare Levi 501s over a black lace body suit, a shredded Transgender Nation T-shirt with the neck and sleeves cut out, a pink triangle, quartz crystal pendant, grunge metal jewellery, and a six-inch long marlin hook dangling around my neck on a length of heavy stainless steel chain' (Stryker 1999: 2). There are, of course, social flows involved in transgender identity that are the subject of heated discussion in feminist and transgender debates that I do not here address.

DOI: 10.3366/E1750224108000366

Becoming-Woman: A Flight into Abstraction

Gillian Howie   University of Liverpool

Abstract

In this paper I argue that the idea 'becoming-woman' is an attempt to transform embodied experience but, because it is unable to concern itself with mechanisms, structures and processes of sexual differentiation, fails in this task. In the first section I elaborate the relationship between becoming-woman and Deleuze's 'superior' or 'transcendental' empiricism and suggest that problems can be traced back to an underlying Humean empiricism. Along with Hume, Deleuze, it seems, presumes a bundle model of the object which dissolves things into episodic objects of perception and leaves the subject unable to distinguish between fanciful objects, erroneous perception and any other thing. The empiricist ontology thus has consequences for epistemology and leaves us unable to question the conservative tendencies of common sense. As an alternative to transcendental empiricism, the second section considers how transcendental realism, with its ontological commitment to the mind-independent character of things, may provide a more fruitful and productive line of enquiry. Given that there is such a choice, in the third section I speculate as to the specific desires that drive such philosophical abstraction; abstraction which culminates in the non sex-specific figure becoming-woman whilst disguising the mind-independent character of the mechanisms, structures and objects that affect the subject. So I conclude that, despite all appearances of radicalism, the philosophical model 'becoming-woman' – aligned as it is with schizo-processes and the philosophical loss of mind-independent things – is more of the same and sexual difference remains a hidden term. Due to this, I believe that feminists should view it with suspicion.

Keywords: abstraction, becoming-woman, body-without-organs, feminism, schizo-processes, sexual difference, transcendental empiricism, transcendental realism, Deleuze, Bhaskar, Jameson.

The figure 'becoming-woman' is often associated with *A Thousand Plateaus* but first appears in the first volume of the Capitalism and Schizophrenia series: *Anti-Oedipus*. The *Anti-Oedipus* was written during a time reverberating from the impact of the revolt of 1968.[1] Exploding the liberal myths of stability and integration, the noisy events of 1968 forced an epistemic and philosophical shift (Buchanan 2000: 13).[2] Deleuze describes May 1968 as an 'intempestif': an untimely irruption of pure virtuality (Conley 2000: 22). Accordingly, 'event 1968' signifies a rupture when, for a moment, there was a sense of life replete with new beginnings and potential 'becomings'. Between this moment and the reestablishment of Gaullist political order is the figure 'becoming-woman' which, alongside 'becoming-animal' and 'becoming-imperceptible', reveals a view of life as indeterminate creative process.

If a Deleuzian event signals a moment of productive intensity, a process without determinate outcome whereby new possibilities are revealed, then the association not just with affirmative becoming but also, and specifically, with becoming-*woman* requires – and has received – special attention. Where 'becoming' is the actualisation of an immanent encounter between forces, becoming-woman is supposed to mark degrees of intensities and states. Becoming-woman should thus be construed as a topological position, as a line of flight, a passage that by-passes empirical women (Braidotti 2005: 303). Indeed, working in the abstract, 'becoming-woman' stands with 'becoming-animal' and 'becoming-imperceptible' as a form of minoritarian-becoming. But there seems little to say about the peculiarities of becoming-*woman* rather than, say, becoming-insect.

The transformation of identities so envisaged is clearly not the same as that envisaged in calls for emancipation and liberation; the blood pulsating through the macro-political enlightenment project of feminism. There are two main differences between, what might be called, the macro political project of feminism and the micro process 'becoming-woman'. The first difference concerns the nature of goal-oriented activity. By defining 'becoming' as indeterminate, Deleuze attempts to signal numerous possible outcomes given in an event. It could be argued that the feminist project closes down all but those that fit with modern ideas of rights. While I remain unconvinced about this, as there are as many outcomes for the feminist project as there are feminists, it is the case that just about all feminisms posit a system whereby one identifiable group, men, benefit from the oppression of another group, women. Whether this is presented in psychoanalytic, sociological or economic terms, there remains an underlying philosophical commitment to some form of identity and a political commitment to changing that state of affairs. Neither Deleuze nor Guattari would really demur from this, admitting that: 'it is of course indispensable for women to conduct a molar politics with a view to winning back their own organism, their own history, their own subjectivity'.

They continue, however, by warning that it is dangerous to confine oneself to such a subject 'which does not function without drying up a spring or stopping a flow'. Their comparison between such a dried up molar subject and a molecular 'becoming-woman' takes me to the second main difference. Within recent feminist theory, the 'body' has gained a privileged theoretical position. As Sara Ahmed notes, this is probably because feminist theory has identified the association of reason with masculinity and femininity with the body as the condition for the exclusion of women from theoretical enquiry and marginalisation from public discourse (Ahmed 2000: 40). As a response to such sex-based dimorphism, there has been a tendency within feminist theory to return to phenomenological analysis in order to rethink the body as something which is neither given in nature nor as a separate substance from mind. In a similar vein, becoming-woman focuses attention on the body but, and here lies the second main difference, becoming-woman requires us to reconstruct the physical body of macro-political movements into a 'body-without-organs'.

The body-without-organs is the virtual dimension of the body, with all the potential connections, affects and movements.[3] In order to reconstruct the physical body in this way we are encouraged to abstract relations of movement and rest, speed and slowness and emission of particles from the body (Deleuze and Guattari 1987: 276). Abstraction here is not supposed to be the work of reason but, instead, to indicate a material process. And this is the point of contention. While becoming-woman may focus critical attention on the historical and socially structured quality of bodies, this move into abstraction could equally well be described as *dis*embodiment, and disembodiment is arguably at odds with any productive and beneficial social critique of invested desire. It certainly seems a long way from feminist phenomenology which looks to explore how (inter)subject experience is lived and felt in the flesh.

In her paper 'Discontinuous Becomings,' Rosi Braidotti (1993) helpfully articulates the problem that concerns me here. Deleuze postulates a general 'becoming-woman' and simultaneously fails to take into account the historical and epistemological specificity of the female feminist standpoint: it is a theory of difference with no room for sexual difference (Braidotti 1993: 42). Rather than becoming-woman resulting in the dissolution of identities, where new forms and connections might emerge, this process of becoming seems to be 'sex specific, sexually differentiated and take different forms according to different gendered sex-positions' (Braidotti 1993: 52). I believe that Braidotti is right to suspect that the idea 'becoming-woman' empties out the idea of sexual difference but also, I maintain, manages to reintroduce sexual difference, silently, through the back door.

The problem, I contend, lies in the tension between the wish to transform embodied experience and the means by which this is thought. Whether or not becoming-woman is a flight from the specificity of any particular body as engaged with other living bodies, or is a way to disorganise the socially-structured body, it *is* the case that the alignment of becoming-woman with schizo-processes catches women in an epistemic bind. I shall be arguing that this theoretical model not only naturalises social principles of organisation but also removes critical epistemic tools. Thus, despite all appearances of radicalism, the philosophical model is unable to offer any practical insights and feminists should view it with suspicion.

Object Lost

In *Empiricism and Subjectivity* we find elaborated the empirical principles of immanence and experiment, which are key features of the 'positive ontology' expressed in the leitmotif becoming-woman (Sotirin 2005: 99). Indeed, Deleuze's transcendental empiricism, famously formulated in *Difference and Repetition*, has its origins in this study of Hume. There is much to be said about Hume's empiricism and its influence on Deleuze, but Rajchman manages to distil four themes from *Empiricism and Subjectivity* that inform Deleuze's later work. These themes are: the idea of probability replacing that of necessity, the idea of creative experimentation, the idea that the self is not given but formed and the claim that apparently mind-independent identities are actually dependent on the intercession of images, passions and ideas (Rajchman 2000: 6–7, 17). All these themes evolve from the primary claim that complex ideas or impressions are formed from simple ones which are associated according to principles of the imagination. Because all ideas can be traced back to sense experience and ideas are brought together by the imagination, Deleuze believes that he can discern an empiricist path to experiment and creativity. Because the idea of 'becoming-woman' requires us to follow this empiricist path,

I believe that we can trace back some of the problems with 'becoming-woman' to the conceptual distinctions first found in Hume's empiricism and, specifically, in Deleuze's reading of Hume. I am interested in how the social - patriarchal - organisation of experience is mystified and, in order to explore this, I shall concentrate on the confusion between real and fanciful objects of experience within both Hume and Deleuze's empiricism.

Eugene Holland detects a change in emphasis between the *Anti-Oedipus* and a *Thousand Plateaus* and notes that the optimism of the former gives way to a slightly more hesitant portrayal of the relationship of desire to the body-without-organs in the latter (Holland 60). In the latter, wishing to avoid either 'over-coagulation' or 'wild chaos', Deleuze and Guattari develop the idea of a difference-engine: a body-without-organs continually forming and reforming passionate attachments (Deleuze and Guattari 1988: 61). Returning to this either-or in *What is Philosophy*, they suggest that we need a little Humean order to protect us from slipping into the fantastical chaos of madness (Deleuze and Guattari 1994: 201). I am interested in the relationship between the apparently welcome loss of the 'object a' in a *Thousand Plateaus* – a joyful deliverance from fixation on any naturally, socially or neurotically imposed object or activity – and the protective Humean rules which reign in our most fantastical ideas. There is much of interest in *Empiricism and Subjectivity*, not least the account of passion in relation to belief, but I shall have to restrict the scope of this paper in order to explore whether a demarcation between 'real' and 'fanciful' ideas can make sense without the idea of a mind-independent object of some sort. I shall return to a distinction between object and thing in the next section when I investigate whether Roy Bhaskar has anything to contribute to the idea of a minor science.

In *Empiricism and Subjectivity* Deleuze affirms the conceptual machinery of the *Treatise* and *Enquiry*.[4] According to Deleuze, the given is the idea as it is in the mind, without anything transcending it (Deleuze 1991: 28). This certainly resonates with Hume's assertion that we are only ever immediately acquainted with the content of our own perceptions, indeed 'to hate, to love, to think, to feel, to see; all this is nothing but to perceive' (Hume 1978: 1.1.V1). In *A Treatise of Human Nature* Hume divides perceptions into impressions and ideas, distinguished only by force and liveliness. Impressions are the first appearance of mental content and ideas are derivative weaker copies. The difference between ideas and impressions can be summed up as that between experiencing x and thinking about x (Shand 1993: 144). It could thus be said that every perception appears both as an impression and an idea and every simple idea can be traced back to an impression.[5]

However, there are impressions of sensation and reflection. The first are really sense experiences. The second are new impressions derived from the way we react to sense experience. For this reason we could say that ideas derived from impressions of reflection depend in part on the nature and working of the mind (Hume 1978:1.1.1/2). If an idea derives from an impression of reflection only, then it is not an objective feature of the world but one that depends on our natural propensity to react to experiences in certain ways. Hume argues that perceptions are distinct from each other, that they can exist at different times and that they can be conceived as existing separately without contradiction (Hume 1978: 1.1.3). Therefore any connection, if indeed there is any such, is contingent and not necessary. It is the human mind which, according to certain natural propensities, associates perceptions that have logically distinct existences and between which no necessary connections can be discovered either by reason or observation. This problem of natural necessity as expressed by Hume helps Deleuze develop an account of probability.

Further developing the line of argument which leads from necessity to probability, Deleuze notes the Humean questions: why do I expect B to follow from A, and how can I explain my idea of necessary connection? Sticking close to the Humean analysis of inductive reason, Deleuze's starting position is that all ideas can be traced back to an impression and that each impression is distinct. As 'if A then B' is not an idea of reason (we can always imagine B without A) we have to look to sense experience to give us grounds for our belief. But because we do not perceive a causal relation between A and B the connection has to be explained by something in the perceiver (Williams 2003: 87). For Hume the constant conjunction of ideas (AB) in the past produces a habit in the mind. We infer that where there is an A there will be a B, or where a B there was an A, on the basis of custom which is a subterranean phenomenon (Sedgwick 2001: 24). The distinction then between constant conjunction and necessary connection can only be the force of the expectation. Similarly, according to Deleuze, causality is felt: it is a perception of the mind and not a conclusion of the understanding' (Deleuze 1991: 26). From this he establishes the principle that necessity belongs to the subject only insofar as the subject contemplates and not insofar as it acts.

So, there are impressions and ideas, and ideas are associated according to principles of connection, namely resemblance, contiguity and causation. All complex ideas are derived from a combination of simple ideas and can be divided into three kinds: those concerning relations, modes and substances. Cause, permanence of objects and subject identity are all ideas of reflection: an habitual response to an impression of reflection – itself a (natural) response to sensation. The world as it is described through our beliefs, with objects and subjects that persist over time entering into causal relationships, is a result of associating ideas and impressions according to these principles of association. But because the idea of, say, substance is not traced back to an impression of sense experience it is not an idea of an objective feature in the world.

Identifying the essence of empiricism with the principles of association, Deleuze suggests that empiricism is more a philosophy of the imagination than of the senses. This definition also underlies the distinction between 'simple empiricism' and 'superior empiricism'. The former is mainly concerned with sense impressions and ideas that can be traced to such impressions whilst the latter is directed to the way imagination moves from one idea to another. Through associating ideas, moving from one impression or idea to another, the subject inhabits a world of subjects, objects and causal relations, a world filled with things it has never actually seen or touched. For this reason, the subject could be said to 'transcend' the given (Deleuze 1991: 24). Deleuze goes further than this however. The subject transcends what is given only because it has already experienced constant conjunction. So, Deleuze infers, before there can be belief about the world, the world must have already been organised into a constant, regular, coherent world of common sense.[6]

The roots of transcendental empiricism lie in the distinction Deleuze draws between what we might describe as rationalist and naturalistic transcendentalism. So, when he writes 'nothing is ever transcendental' (Deleuze 1991: 24) he is referring to rationalist transcendentalism. Instead, by giving a naturalist account of the principles of association and by describing the mind as passive, he attempts to give a non–rationalist explanation for how our world of experience transcends, goes beyond, 'the given'. Association, he claims, is a law of nature, defined through its effects rather than known as a cause. As we have seen, even the idea of *necessity* can be traced back to an impression of reflection, which is a feeling of compulsion accompanying the connection of two ideas. The difference between a series considered a case of constant conjunction and a series considered to be necessary lies in the degree of anticipation felt by the perceiver (Deleuze 1991: 68).

That a distinction might be drawn between these two series is significant and strays onto Kantian territory. How do we distinguish between a constant conjunction that indicates causality and one that is merely a long-standing coincidence of AB? Earlier I noted that ideas, which are derived from impressions of reflection, differ from those ideas derived from sensation, with only the latter correlated to objective features of the world. Thus we may have an idea of 'evil' but because there is no correlative impression of sensation we have to trace it back to an impression of reflection: a response to a different impression of sensation. Necessity, likewise, seems to be a projection into the world of an idea of an inner state. The way to distinguish between two beliefs, for example 'the sun will rise tomorrow' and 'this Irishman will not be witty' is not through appealing to an idea of necessity but to experience itself. Repetitions in experience give probable grounds for believing that the sun will rise tomorrow but experience gives no probable grounds for believing that 'this Irishman will not be witty' (Deleuze 1991: 69). The implication of this, for Deleuze, is that we must restrict our speculations to objects as they appear to us through the senses (Deleuze 1991: 88). The object of philosophical probability is supposed to lie in the coherent relationship between habit and experience. For the feminists amongst us, this should already cause some alarm bells to ring.

This relationship between habit and experience does seem to provide us with a number of epistemological tools. First we can question the distinction between fanciful claims to necessary connection and inferences based on probability by pointing out that that there is no impression of sense that corresponds to 'necessity'. We are, though, not left floundering in a skeptical soup because we can, secondly, distinguish between justifiable and unjustifiable beliefs based on probability of past sense experience. But we are left with an ontological problem. To describe that which appears in experience as an 'object' disguises the underlying constructivist ontology: 'without passive synthesis there would be no chair to consider'. Persistence and substance are ideas with no corresponding sense impression.

For both Deleuze and Hume the idea that the world might display any objective (mind-independent) feature is compromised. Throughout the *Treatise*, Hume is at pains to demonstrate the arbitrariness of mechanisms that lead us to believe 'quite falsely, that we are aware directly aware of an external world' (Fogelin 1993: 127). Similarly, Deleuze suggests that the very idea of a thing external to perception, or a mind-independent object, is a contradiction – one that we live with but a contradiction nonetheless. The perceptual object is the only real object

(Deleuze 1991: 88). Along with Hume's philosophical refutation of an independent external world is a refutation of representational realism and causal theories of perception. Arguing against causal theories of perception, Deleuze maintains an empiricist line which is that a 'causal relation' could only exist between two objects in experience whereas causal accounts of perception hold a mind-independent thing responsible for that perception.

The only criterion of truth, the only reason to assent to any view, is a strong inclination to consider that the object *is* as it *appears*. This inclination is explained as a propensity of the imagination worked on by experience and habit; memory and sense. The memory, senses and understanding are, therefore, all of them founded on the imagination, or 'the vivacity of our ideas' (Hume 1978: 1.1V.V11). This strong inclination would explain why we believe, and are justified in so doing, that the sun will rise tomorrow and do not believe that we will encounter a unicorn in the office this afternoon. However, this does seem to confuse rational and causal explanation. An inclination may well be an explanation but it is not itself a reason for believing or assenting. Nor does the invocation of 'inclination' help to explain error: prosaically, we may be inclined – quite wrongly – to believe the stick is bent rather than straight when perceived in water. Less prosaically, if in my experience all women have been responsible for domestic work, made the tea in meetings and been paid less than men for the same work is my belief that 'woman x will (probably) do these things' be legitimate? To put it otherwise, how may we explain that which is perceived as habitual and regular and how may we correct our erroneous expectations?

Of course, appeal to an inner nature will not do. Nor will an appeal to a mind-independent thing help to distinguish between the fanciful idea of a unicorn and the perceptual event, or hallucination, of a unicorn or between the hallucination of a unicorn and the sun. Deleuze argues instead that there is a difference between the fictions of continuous and distinct existence and other imaginative fancies: between ideas of the sun and ideas of unicorns. In the former case, the imagination, he says, does not offer the understanding continuous and distinct existence as objects of possible experience, but this does not mean that the ideas are *merely* fanciful. Instead, he suggests continuous existence is a characteristic of the World in general: 'it is not an object because it is the horizon which every object presupposes' (Deleuze 1991: 80). For the sake of coherence we presuppose, as a principle, that the object of sense, which we only encounter episodically, is a mind-independent thing. That we experience something is not in doubt, its mind-independent nature is a postulation. At the same time, reason acknowledges that the world of mind-independent objects is 'an outright fiction of the imagination', 'a fictive foreign world' but it is a fiction that cannot be corrected. The result is a number of delirious compromises: 'the mind is no longer anything but delirium and madness' (Deleuze 1991: 81).

Because our intellectual grasp of nature has to be corrected according to experience, Deleuze considers the philosophy of experience to be a critique of the philosophy of nature. Yet it is the naturalistic description of the principles of association which allows Deleuze to define the relationship between the transcendental and immanent (Deleuze 2001: 26–8). It is an interesting transcendentalism, however. Deleuze has argued that it is rationalism which (falsely) transfers or projects mental determinations – necessity, truth, universality – to external objects. Because the idea of necessity is a projection onto a series of constant conjunctions, he can introduce radical contingency into his own transcendental argument in two ways. First, any claims about the principles of association can only be probable; second, Deleuze introduces the possibility of radically different experiences. Because there is no (real) basis for regularity – let alone necessity – except habit, there is no direction to future events except that given by sensation.

> In a word we always return to the same conclusion; the given, the mind, the collection of perceptions cannot call upon anything other than themselves. But as it calls upon itself, what exactly is it calling upon, since the collection remains arbitrary, and since every idea and every impression can disappear or be separated from the mind without contradiction? (Deleuze 1991: 89, 90)

His answer is that natural principles of association settle the imagination (Deleuze 2001: 41).

Dismissing *ad hominem* philosophical arguments, Deleuze suggests that an adequate approach to the history of philosophy is not one which criticises philosophical assumptions but rather one which addresses problems as they concern the particular philosopher. Hume was absorbed with the questions about whether or not we could justify our beliefs in necessity, regularity, and causality and, if not, whether we would have to abandon beliefs in the uniformity of nature and scientific experiment. These questions result from a more fundamental philosophical problem: as we have no grounds for believing that which we do not observe, what should we believe and how do we explain the origin of our ideas? We are left asking whether we can say anything meaningful about that which we do not directly perceive or that which is a reaction to that which we perceive. Hume's conclusion is that, for the most part, the fundamental beliefs of ordinary people are either false or unfounded and the philosophers' attempts to 'put anything better in their place is wholly insignificant or unintelligible' (Fogelin 1993: 111).

There is with this sort of empiricism a slip between epistemology and ontology, which is often disguised within phenomenology.[7] The epistemological problems noted above arise from a *metaphysical* presumption that objects can be best understood as a bundle, whether that bundle be of ideas, impressions or perceptions. This bundle model of the object tends to collapse ontological questions (such as those relating to the mind-independent or dependent nature of the thing) into problems arising from the philosophy of perception (objects of sense experience). Objects are re-described merely in terms of how they are perceived: in this case as a succession of distinct and independent perceptions, where every idea could disappear without contradiction (Deleuze 1991: 87, 90).

Object Recovered

When Deleuze recommends concern only with the question of the subject and with the claim that relations are external to ideas, he focuses our attention on the relationship between ontology and epistemology. This ontological commitment to a bundle model of the object tends to reduce things simply to objects of perception. These objects are not considered to be in any meaningful relationship to an external or mind independent 'substantial' thing. Whilst this might play to phenomenologist sensibilities, these particular commitments are more radical and encourage a Deleuzian reading of Hume which first attends to the role of subjectivity in creating the object of perception as a persisting thing and then makes 'the subject' itself a consequence. But we need not take these steps. A philosophical concern with the repetition of resemblances does not need to be a meditation either on the nature of memory or on perception; nor is it, necessarily, a fruitless search for an irretrievably lost object or a recovered trauma. Intuitions can remind reason of its (historicised) blind spots without having to postulate a realm of 'pure difference'.

A helpful comparison can be made between transcendental empiricism and transcendental realism. Both aim to reveal the conditions of events, work through abstraction, investigate the relationship between events and essences or powers and give experimentation a privileged place. Both too might describe themselves within the philosophical history of 'process philosophy'. However, although they are both directed towards disturbing the status quo and reconnecting the subject to their potential – to that which they might become – they differ as to their conception of objects and events; differences which impact on their respective theories of affects. Here I wish merely to suggest possible points of intersection in order to indicate alternative trajectories.

According to the critical realist Roy Bhaskar, Hume's apparent denial of ontology actually results in the generation of an *implicit* ontology and an implicit realism. Commenting on this empiricist realist tradition in *A Realist Theory of Science* Bhaskar claims that the collapse of epistemology into ontology covers or disguises an ontology based on the category of experience, and a form of realism based on the presumed characteristics of objects of experiences, that is, atomistic events and their relations. Hume has, in effect, replaced Locke's ontology of real essences, powers, and atomic constitution with an ontology of impressions (Bhaskar 1975: 40). Hume has also set out an epistemological frame of reference, whereby an analysis of perception and perceived events exhausts our knowledge of nature: that is, our grasp of the world is reduced to sense experience. But the language of 'impression' is really metaphorical: an impression is always an impression 'of something'.

In *Empiricism and Subjectivity* we find nothing that demurs from these fundamental Humean principles and, as we have seen, Deleuze maintains that a number of core beliefs – in mind-independent things, in causal theories of perception, in the continuous and persistent existence of objects – are without proper foundation. Deleuze also considers the distinction between the object (of perception) and the World or Nature to be misleading but unavoidable. Any theory according to which relations are derived from the nature of things is, for Deleuze, non-empiricist. This too is the point of demarcation for Bhaskar but he, unlike Deleuze, develops the idea that relations and powers can ultimately be traced back to (mind-independent) entities.

All versions of realism embrace the claim that what can be said to exist is not confined to that which can be displayed to the senses, or to that which appears as empirical data. That said, Bhaskar's critical realism is not to be strictly identified either with external realism or scientific realism. The former holds the view that the World (reality or universe) exists independently from our beliefs, ideas about it and the impression it makes on us. Scientific realism extends this to the independence of theoretical objects. Bhaskar's critical realism argues that structures and mechanisms exist independently of events and experience (Kaidesoja 2005: 30). Crucially, these mechanisms and structures can explain the events or particular experiences – an explanatory route denied to the Humean.

Critical realism, in particular, is grounded in categories of entities that are characterised by their powers. As Rom Harré notes, the fact that power is not observable in itself but only in its effects is, as Thomas Reid pointed out two hundred and fifty years ago, not an adequate ground for throwing it out as an ontological concept (Harré 2001: 23). Although disagreeing with Harré as to what sort of things can have powers, the efficacy of power is central to Bhaskar's realist theory of science. But these are powers of enduring and transfactually acting things. Realist ontology is thing – rather than event – centered. For Bhaskar things may include powers, forces, mechanisms, characteristics or sets of relations (Bhaskar 1975: 226). These things possess characteristics and tendencies to interact in particular ways with other things. Further, a tendency is more than a power (Bhaskar 1975: 230). It depends upon distinguishing from within that class of actions naturally possible for a thing (in virtue of its being the kind of thing that it is) those that are characteristic of the thing. It is the function of this idea of tendency to individuate natures within kinds, species within genera, individuals within classes etc.

Bhaskar begins by asking: 'what must reality be like in order to make (scientific) experimentation an intelligible activity? (Bhaskar 1975:23). Whereas Deleuze separates realms into the real, virtual and actual, Bhaskar distinguishes between the real, the actual and the empirical: (i) the empirical world is what we experience, the limit of reality according to restrictive forms of empiricism present in the positivist approaches to science; (ii) the actual domain is the realm of events, not all of which are experienced by people; (iii) the real is the domain of the generative mechanisms or structures responsible for events, but which are themselves *unobservable*. Transcendental realist ontology includes specific claims about the ontological structure of the world. Events are certainly not deductively predictable: 'a stray bullet', 'an unhappy childhood affecting the course of history'. However, Bhaskar posits an analytic distinction between a pattern of events and the basis of causal laws – understood as powers of things – inhering in the things themselves as tendencies (117). Unobservable structures and generative mechanisms can generate, but exist independently of, the experience and patterns of events. These can become objects of scientific research; which means that transcendental knowledge of structures is possible. Science attempts to discern the nature of these things, to identify characteristics and tendencies of interaction. Because interaction is not invariant, scientific laws are best understood as explication of tendencies. Causal powers of things are real features of the world. Kind terms, defined in terms of resemblances, are not assemblages – if by assemblage we mean a loose (and subjective) grouping together.

The Humean Deleuze certainly sheds light on the role of habit, demonstrating that the problem of transcendence disappears if the present is in itself a continual state of creative renewal. But in order to establish this, Deleuze makes use of a transcendental argument and appeals to an idea of pure difference. This pure idea of difference functions as a dummy concept. Michael Ayers suggests that Locke's concept of substance is also a dummy concept that can help to explain co–existing sensible qualities. Although such concepts cannot be derived either from reflection or from sensation, it is still not illegitimate to use them to the extent that they help to explain what is sensed by reference to something else, in this case underlying causes. One consequence of using a dummy concept of substance, in the way that Bhaskar does, is that one can accept the self–directed quality of transcendental arguments without also being forced into idealism; indeed one can develop a thoroughly naturalised account.

Both Deleuze and Bhaskar attempt to naturalise Kant's transcendental argument. But whereas Deleuze naturalises it through naturalising the synthetic act and the principles according to which the action is performed, Bhaskar uses arguments that combine *a posteriori* premises and a priori transcendental reasoning (Kaiesoja 2005: 45). Bhaskar assumes both the intelligibility of science and our ability to justify *a priori* the claim that it is a necessary condition of the possibility of certain (located) scientific practices (such as experimentation) and that the ontological structure of the world contains certain features (structures and mechanisms) that are ontologically independent of any pattern of events (Bhaskar 1975: 32). Although necessity is interpreted in a rather Kantian way, he does not posit a bundle model of the object, and so the object of perception as a thing in the world retains a degree of independence from the subject. As Kaidesoja points out whereas concepts are for Kant subject-sided they are, for Bhaskar, object-sided (Kaidesoja 2005:34).

Deleuze relies on a working distinction between the World and beliefs about that world, between states of affairs and propositions, but is unable to account for this 'workability' or coherence except in terms of transcendental doubling.[8] The Humean suggestion, that only a psychological attitude demarcates the fanciful object of perception (unicorns) from the (fanciful) object of perception (substance or mind independent object), not only has little explanatory force but also commits us to a passive subject merely responding to the given: indeed, without being able to account for that given. I am not suggesting that the critical realist contribution to social science is straight–forward, but, if the philosophical arguments are found at least in part convincing then given the similar trajectories as identified at the beginning of this section, a positive way forward could be to explore intersections between critical realism and process philosophy. Bhaskar's distinction between mechanisms (powers) and events might be a helpful way to approach Deleuze's virtual; a comparison between the Real and the Virtual, singularities and powers. Such a productive comparison may be able to retain the spirit of creative transition and combine it with a commitment to social scientific research: a commitment required by feminists. In the current context it may be illuminating to consider what happens when the object is claimed for a (passive) subject, who is unable to tell the difference between fanciful and (fanciful) objects of perception.

Becoming-Woman

In the introduction I suggested that there is a tension between the desire to transform embodied experience and the means by which this is thought. In the first section I elaborated the means by which it is thought as 'superior' or transcendental empiricism. The second section offered transcendental realism as an alternative to transcendental empiricism. The focal point has been that 'becoming-woman' is defined in terms of schizo-processes and schizo-processes depend on the empiricist philosophy of experimentation. Empiricism presumes a bundle model of the object, which dissolves things into episodic objects of perception and leaves the subject unable to distinguish between fanciful and any other object. Despite all the talk about materialism and empiricism the thing – or mind-independent character of the object – disappears. Repeating the Copernican moment, objects become fanciful affects of the subject. In this section I consider the psychology behind the philosophical loss of the mind-independent object and I allow myself to speculate as to the specific desires that drive such philosophical abstraction; abstraction which culminates in the non sex-specific figure 'becoming-woman'.

In psychoanalytic theory, schizophrenia is considered to be a response to a frustrating external world, an instinctual flight in which energy cathexis is withdrawn from external objects. Deleuze and Guattari do not eulogise this clinical condition of schizophrenia, indeed they consider it to be a pathological response to a specific configuration of capital. For Deleuze and Guattari, schizophrenic pathology reveals something profound about the relationship between desire and the social production of identities (subject and object), a relationship which becomes more conspicuous in times of social upheaval, or 'decoding' and 'deterritorialisation', and most obvious during particular stages of capitalist development. In response to the limits of and closures within late capitalism the individual withdraws and ends up as a clinical entity; catatonic and unproductive.

But Deleuze|Guattari still do insist that processes can be adequately described as *schizo*-processes. According to Holland Deleuze|Guattari assign the name 'schizophrenia' to desiring-production in its absolute indeterminate free-state (Holland 2005: 57). For Lambert, although it is a term to be mobilised more within critical theory than clinical practice, it is also indicates 'the orphan unconscious' (Lambert 2000: 139). The unconscious is not to be understood as a kind of theatre where a self is staged and performed through a series of imaginary identifications but, instead, as a productive process. Indeed they describe schizophrenia as an intense and pure process where singularities are brought together in a machinic assemblage and take schizophrenic experiences of unbearable intensities to be the primary level of experience. Intensities are defined in terms of delirium; the result of tension brought about by exterior relations (Goodchild 1996: 84).

Whether they are postulating an ürground of desire[9] or investigating how psychic and social production are manifested in a schizophrenic's delirium, or trying to express schizophrenic experience, the critical method they deploy carries all the hallmarks of clinical schizophrenia. 'Becoming-woman' is one element of this 'schizophrenic thought' where ideas are liberated from the model of logic and words behave like bodies: as asignifying or machinic – material substance(s) (Goodchild 1996: 85). According to Goodchild, the real schizo is someone who temporarily enters into a process, a transition, or a voyage in intensity. 'Schizophrenia is a move to a different quality of consciousness: the *fantasy* of desiring-production' (1996: 90).

Discussing Freud's case of Judge Schreber in the *Anti-Oedipus*, Deleuze|Guattari write that Schreber did not *hallucinate* the experience of becoming-woman and being impregnated by God but rather it was a lived experience: 'the actual lived emotion of having breasts does not resemble breasts, it does not represent them ... nothing but bands of intensity, potentials, thresholds, gradients' (Deleuze and Guattari 1984: 19).[10] There is no distinction to be drawn between that which is real and that which is experienced as real. The idea shifts but only slightly in a *Thousand Plateaus,* where they insist that 'becoming–woman' is an experience that men and women can have (Deleuze and Guattari 1988: 275); although it is an affect which can destabilise dominant identities, molar forms and relations and, arguably, empirical women are more likely to experience (pass through) these bands of intensities. Just why empirical women are more likely to become-woman is without explanation, unless, of course, women are more delirious, perhaps even slightly hysterical.

The description of these processes as schizophrenic is a nudge back to Freud. However for both Freud and Melanie Klein although hallucinations are experienced *as* real they can be distinguished *from* the real. The subject acquires and requires an ability to distinguish between object relations over-determined by particular traumatic memories and object relations that conform to objective demands. But the schizophrenic condition is where words predominate over things. Substitution is not based on resemblance between things but between words that are used to express them: a form of expression where the concrete thing is taken *as though* it were abstract.

Deleuze and Guattari's eulogy to abstraction involves the loss of the concrete object and the appropriation of the World to the subject. If we combine this with the textual absence of any real way to figure the parent–child relationship – which is neither Oedipal nor an arbitrary assemblage – we are reminded of the Freudian description of the origin of psychotic cathectic withdrawal from the object as a narcissistic neurotic denial of mother-other. Irigaray describes this move in the context of transcendental idealism as 'copula without copulation' (Irigaray 1985: 184). It begins to look as though 'becoming-woman' is a sadistic reincorporation into the same. Goodchild then is right, it is a fantasy but more a phantastical move that deflects from formal questions about the relationships between peculiar and specialised abstractions of what we used to call capitalism and patriarchy and how they can be found in cultural texts.

Although 'becoming-woman' is privileged over masculine narcissistic identity in Deleuze and Guattari's work, philosophical abstraction allows sexual difference to be a hidden term. The obvious problems, that women must 'become-woman' and the role played by the motif girl, can be overlooked; we are happy to be that forgiving to many philosophers. But the suspicion is that there is something more profound and structural.[11] Addressing this, whilst commenting on Deleuze's remark that eating bored him', Nicole Shukin investigates *A Thousand Plateaus* and discovers that Deleuze and Guattari dichotomise nomadology (the raw: intense) and the regulatory (the domestic) (Shukin 2000:147). This does seem to be an old-fashioned duality between nature (power: movement of the infinite: the involuntary) and convention, where convention is judged according to ethical criteria discerned in nature. There appears, as Jerry Fleiger notes (2000: 40) a worn-out essentialism here, an association of the non-subjectified woman, nature, flows, springs, excess, difference, differences even gaps and tears – the very underbelly of enlightened modern reason. Women, then, are of interest (to whom?): 'only in their capacity to quicken the blood; carriers of strange winds and estrangement that provide Western man with the conduit he needs to abdicate himself' (Shukin 2000: 148).

These familiar dualisms do indicate something about the movement of the text which is disguised in the abstraction associated with schizo-processes. More profound, I believe, is the way in which the empiricism attempts to neutralise experience under the guise of introducing passion and affect. The bundle model of the object reduces things to episodic objects of perception and, in the end, throws the weight of objectivity onto the subject. If the principles of association, external to their terms, are actually *social* principles of organisation, there is something ominous about the description of regularity as the result of passive contraction. The suspicion that Deleuze opens the philosophical space to elide the natural and social is confirmed by his own description of the supposedly 'natural' principles of association: 'The moral problem is the problem of schematism, that is the act by means of which we refer the natural interests to the political category of the whole or to the totality that is not given in nature...The moral is the system of means which allow my particular interest, and also the interest of the other, to be satisfied and realized' (Deleuze 1991: 40–1). This point is also made clearly in his later essay on Hume: 'What is called a theory of association finds its direction and its truth in a casuistry of relations, a practice of law, of politics, of economics, that completely changes the nature of philosophical reflection' (Deleuze 2001: 36).

But we have to ask whether the empiricist philosopher, even a philosopher of superior empiricism, is able to distinguish between the natural and social clearly enough to demarcate the origin of the principles, the conditions of an event, or to identify whose desires are being satisfied. The empiricist slip between ontology and epistemology disguises the mind-independent character of the mechanisms, structures and objects affecting the subject whilst undermining our ability to say anything about them. Any proposition has as much status as any other '(in my experience) women are hysterical' because justification remains at the surface: how it appears to particular subjects and according to (their) desires, experience and, indeed, interests. This problem is especially acute where the philosophical move not only undermines our ability to respond to the question 'in whose interests?', but also dissolves the very integrity of other subjects.[12] Gender remains latent in the text of A Thousand Plateaus because the abstraction, that is the schizophrenic move, drops things and so the context of the idea or the affective intensity from sight. Deleuze expresses boredom with eating because he can take it for granted (Shukin 2000: 148). The labor of women and our actual, embroiled lives are sacrificed in the text.

Conclusion

The concept 'becoming-woman' has obvious heuristic potential. The idea that becoming can be a process which is not governed by a stable centralised self who somehow manages to supervise their own unfolding (Braidotti 2005: 303) expresses a way to release (the thought of) identity from dualistic and hierarchical constraints of a 'normalised', organised and thoroughly social body. The alignment of becoming-woman with schizo-processes indicates how subject identity might be more mobile if it were free from the (psychic) constraints of oedipal organisation and the legal and moral constraints of an overregulated social world But the interrogation of Deleuze's superior empiricism must raise a question about the therapeutic value of a philosophy of affect, unable to address itself to the context or location of the affect, of a philosophy of event, unable to address itself to the conditions of the event, and of a philosophy of becoming unable to tell the difference between fantastical objects and mind-independent objects.

Unlike Deleuze and Guattari, Fredric Jameson believes that schizophrenia is primarily a social and political condition whereby reference is confused, ideas come to stand for objects, each idea is presumed interchangeable with others and concrete things are taken as though they were abstract. It actually marks the cultural condition of late (developed) capitalism in which the loss of the real object contributes to social and political confinement.[13] According to Jameson, in late capitalism, the monadic – rather than nomadic – subject can no longer look directly for the referent in the real world but must, as the subjects in Plato's Cave, trace mental images of the world on confining walls (Jameson 3). For Jameson, then, there is nothing inherently redemptive about schizo- processes; indeed the loss of objects in the process of abstraction poses and disguises real threats to the subject. The most that can be hoped for within postmodernism is that subjects can grasp this schizophrenic confinement and this can shock them out from Plato's Cave.

When mind-independence is described as fanciful and persisting identity as a consequence of subject involvement then to all intents and purposes objects disappear. Here we can see a slip between empiricism and idealism/rationalism (Zizek 2004: 22; Howie 2002: 2, 206). But as we know by now, ideas and objects are not the same thing and mind-independent objects only disappear from philosophical discourse. The belief in immediacy concedes the very principles of containment and closure it was mobilised to break apart, so that the longed-for outbreak is an outbreak into the mirror. Unless these things are recovered in theory, it will be more difficult to resist patriarchal organisation of difference and becoming-woman will not trigger a new plane but remain the same: phantastical self-creation.

There is a sense in which Deleuze plays across two surfaces: a Nietzschean/Heideggerian critique of reasoning in the name of 'unreason' (Lewis Carroll/Artaud) and a critique of bourgeois rationality in the name of 'another' (molar/molecular). The aesthetic space between discursive barbarism (logical positivism) and poetic euphemism (utopianism) is one into which the philosopher can burrow. But the idea that *all* becomings are minoritarian and *will* unsettle the status quo is one side of that movement: utopic. It is premised on an economic model of the psyche that proposes a theory of circulation of intensities: a kind of redemption that eliminates mediation. Deleuze writes that some ideas, such as becoming-woman, should be seen as governing principles; as schemas or rules of construction. Yet the true nature of the schematism might be ultimately revealed as the interest of gendered industrial society – where things are apprehended through the process of manufacture and administration; productive assemblages where everything is converted into repeatable replaceable units or blocks and labour segregated by race, sex and class.

Let us return to the problem of transcendence reconfigured as states of renewal. The problem expressed in Deleuze's semiotics is to make sense, sense that is more closely related to nonsense than propositional sense, and so make thinkable what we have not yet been able to think, to make visible that which we have been unable to discern (Rajchman 2000: 67). In this case, how may we think outside the perimeter of sex/gender? Trying to do something similar, whilst keeping in mind the dangers of abstraction, Theodor Adorno writes that nothing can be experienced as living if it does not contain a promise of a creative transition, which at its heart suggests an impossibility of thinking that which nevertheless must be thought (Adorno 1988: 145). The new in this way shudders along and this shuddering response to the new is both a reaction to the cryptically shut, which is a function of indeterminacy, and a reaction to abstraction. The abstraction of the new is bound with – but not reducible to – the commodity character; an aesthetic seal of expanded reproduction with its promise of undiminished plenitude. If the new itself becomes a fetish there is usually a problem between new means and old ends (Adorno 1997: 21–3). In this case, because the means remain the same (social principles of association), the end is already predictable (reterritorialisation). The problem of means and ends, unthinkable without an idea of the object, can affect a falling-back into the ever-same.

Becoming-woman suggests a radically androgynous transvaluation of values, and it certainly appears to leap over the risk of dimorphic essentialism in an un-gendered becoming. It does so by risking, instead, de-contextualising and appropriating the affective body; interning the same dimorphic values whilst cutting the ground from critical interjection. The welcome idea that each moment already contains creative transition, immanent transcendence, opens the future to radical contingency. But the idea of 'becoming something else' is neither innocent nor without context. Immanent transcendence was figured by Deleuze in his interview with Parnet as a holy trinity: Brain (god/concept), marrow (son/affect), tongue (holy spirit/percept). My shudder, an affective response to the place from which I speak, is that the brain, the marrow and the tongue, might figure another – and the same – holy trinity.

References

Adorno, Theodor W. (1997) *Aesthetic Theory*, trans. Robert Hullot-Kentor, London: Althone Press, 1997.

Adorno, Theodor W. (2000) *Metaphysics: Concept and Problems*, trans. Edward Jephcott, Cambridge: Polity.

Ahmed, Sara (2000) *Strange Encounters: Embodied Others in Post-Coloniality*. London: Routledge.

Bhaskar, Roy (1975) *A Realist Theory of Science*, London: Verso.

Braidotti, Rosi (1993) 'Discontinuous Becoming', *Journal of the British Society for Phenomenology*, 24.1 (1993) pp. 44–54.

Braidotti, Rosi (2005) 'Woman', in *The Deleuze Dictionary*, ed. Adrian Parr, Edinburgh: Edinburgh University Press.

Buchanan, Ian, and Claire, Colebrook (eds) (2000) *Deleuze and Feminist Theory*, Edinburgh: Edinburgh University Press.

Buchanan, Ian (2000) *Deleuzism: A Metacommentary*, Edinburgh: Edinburgh University Press.

Conley, Verena Andermatt (2000) 'Becoming-Woman: Now', in Ian Buchanan and Claire Colebrook (eds), *Deleuze and Feminist Theory*, Edinburgh: Edinburgh University Press, pp. 18–37.

Deleuze, Gilles (1990) *Expressionism in Philosophy: Spinoza*, trans. Martin Joughan, New York: Zone Books.

Deleuze, Gilles (1991) *Empiricism and Subjectivity: An Essay on Hume's Theory of Human Nature*, trans. Constantin Boundas, New York: Columbia University Press [Preface 1989].

Deleuze, Gilles (1997) *Difference and Repetition*, trans. Paul Patton, London: Athlone Press.

Deleuze, Gilles and Félix Guattari (1984) *Anti-Oedipus: Capitalism and Schizophrenia 1*, trans. Robert Hurley, Mark Seem, Helen Lane, London: Athlone Press.

Deleuze, Gilles (1988) *A Thousand Plateaus: Capitalism and Schizophrenia 2*. trans. Brian Massumi, London: Athlone Press.

Deleuze, Gilles (2001) *Pure Immanence: Essays on a Life*, trans. Anne Boyman, New York: Zone Books.

Deleuze, Gilles and Félix Guattari (1994) *What is Philosophy?*, trans. Hugh Tomlinson and Graham Burchell, New York: Columbia University Press.

Fleiger, Jerry Aline (2000) 'Becoming-Woman: Deleuze, Schreber and Molecular Identification', in Ian Buchanan and Claire Colebrook (eds) *Deleuze and Feminist Theory*, Edinburgh: Edinburgh University Press, pp. 38–63.

Fogelin, Robert (1993) 'Hume's Scepticism', in *The Cambridge Companion to Hume*, ed. David Norton, Cambridge: Cambridge University Press.

Goodchild, Philip (1996) *Deleuze and Guattari: An Introduction to the Politics of Desire*, London: Sage.

Harré, Rom and Roy, Bhaskar (2001) 'How to Change Reality: Story vs. Structure', in *After Postmodernism: An Introduction to Critical Realism,* ed. José López and Garry Potter, London: Athlone Press.

Holland, Eugene (2005) 'Desire', in Charles Stivale (ed.), *Gilles Deleuze: Key Concepts*, Bucks: Acumen, pp 53–62.

Howie, Gillian (2002) *Deleuze and Spinoza: Aura of Expressionism*, Basingstoke: Palgrave.

Hume, David (1970) *Enquiries Concerning the Human Understanding and Concerning the Principles of Morals*, ed. Lewis A. Selby-Bigge, Oxford: Clarendon Press.

Hume, David (1978) *A Treatise on Human Nature*, ed. Lewis A. Selby-Bigge, Oxford: Clarendon Press.

Irigaray, Luce (1985) *Speculum of the Other Woman*, trans. Gillian Gill, Ithaca: Cornell University Press.

Jameson, Frederic (1988) *The Cultural Turn: Selected Writings on the Postmodern 1983–1998*, London: Verso.

Kaidesoja, Tuukka (2005) 'The Trouble with Transcendental Arguments: Towards a Naturalisation of Roy Bhaskar's Early Realist Ontology', *Journal of Critical Realism*. 4. 1, pp. 28–61.

Kaufman, Eleanor (2000) 'Towards a Feminist Philosophy of Mind', in Ian Buchanan and Claire Colebrook (eds), *Deleuze and Feminist Theory*, Edinburgh: Edinburgh University Press, pp. 128–43.

Lambert, Gregg (2000) 'On the Uses and Abuses of Literature for Life', in Ian Buchanan and John Marks (eds), *Deleuze and Literature*, Edinburgh: Edinburgh University Press, pp. 135–66.

Lorraine, Tamsin (1999) *Irigaray and Deleuze: Experiments in Visceral Philosophy*, Ithaca and London: Cornell University Press.

Olkowski, Dorothea, (2000) 'Morpho-logic in Deleuze and Irigaray', in Ian Buchanan and Claire Colebrook (eds), *Deleuze and Feminist Theory*, Edinburgh: Edinburgh University Press, pp. 86–109.

Paretti, Jonah (1996) 'Capitalism and Schizophrenia; contemporary Visual Culture and Acceleration of Identity Formation/Dissolution', *Negations: Interdisciplinary Journal of Social Thought*, Winter.

Rajchman, John (2000) *The Deleuze Connections*, Cambridge, MA: MIT Press.

Sedgwick, Peter (2001) *Descartes to Derrida: An Introduction to European Philosophy*, Oxford: Blackwell.

Shand, John (1993) *Philosophy and Philosophers: an Introduction to Western Philosophy*, London: UCL Press.

Shukin, Nicole (2000) 'Deleuze and Feminisms: Involuntary Regulators and Affective Inhibitors', in Ian Buchanan and Claire Colebrook (eds), *Deleuze and Feminist Theory*, Edinburgh: Edinburgh University Press, pp. 144–55.

Sotirin, Patty (2005) 'Becoming-Woman', in *Gilles Deleuze: Key Concepts*, ed. Charles Stivale, Bucks: Acumen, 2005, pp. 98–109.

Tauchert, Ashley (2005) 'Against Transgression', *Critical Quarterly*, 47(3), pp. 1–11.

Williams, James (2003) *Gilles Deleuze's Difference and Repetition*, Edinburgh: Edinburgh University Press.

Zizek, Slavoj (2004) *Organs without Bodies. On Deleuze and Consequences*, New York and London: Routledge.

Notes

An earlier version of this paper will be appearing as 'Becoming-Woman: the brain, marrow, the tongue or copula without copulation' in Deleuzian Events: Writing lHistory ed H Berressem and L. Hakerkamp (Hamburg: Lit 2008)

1. The connection between becoming-woman and the events of 1968 is made by Conley in *Becoming-Woman Now*. In 1968 Deleuze also began to teach in the experimental department of philosophy of the University of Paris at Vincennes.

2. This point is made clearly by Michel Foucault in the Preface to Schizophrenia and Capitalism.

3. The BwOs is also defined as a recording surface which functions according to a disjunctive syntheses and as a surface which is inscribed containing both what is inscribed and the energy that inscribes it (AO 78, 327). See also Buchanan 147.

4. In his essay on Hume in *Pure Immanence* Deleuze considers the principal difference to lie between ideas/impressions and principles of association rather than between ideas and impressions of reflection and sensation.

5. This idea could support claims made in *Expressionism* (Deleuze 1990) that in some sense a mode is in – or a modification of – both the attribute of thought and the attribute of extension. However it raises similar problems, for instance, is it the case that whenever I think about the day I broke my hand I experience it?

6. By making nature or mind the condition for the uniformity of nature, Deleuze does seem to address the more sceptical elements of Hume's empiricism but only at the cost of engaging more directly with transcendental argument.

7. It is exactly this problem that Jean-Paul Sartre addresses in the Introduction to *Being and Nothingness*.

8. This is resolved in *Expressionism* through the parallelism, but the parallelism itself depends on a number of rationalist principles to get off the ground.

9. This would be supported by the claim that the unconscious belongs to the realm of physics and that the BwOs and its intensities are not metaphors but matter (AO: 283)

10. Fleiger (2000), referencing David Santer, draws out potential socio-political connections between the molecular (or minoritarian) and becoming-woman through an analysis of Freud's own account of investment in the social field. Although suggestive, this still requires a tougher realism than that afforded by Deleuze's empiricism (49).

11. This same issue makes an appearance in Deleuze's work on Spinoza see Howie 2002: 181–5.

12. Questions concerning the role of theory intersect with questions concerning the mind as it is figured in feminist discourse, especially in relation to the body. There is a nice clear exposition of this in Kaufman (2000: 135).

13. For a comparison between Jameson and Deleuze Guattari see Buchanan pp. 158–62 and Paretti.

DOI: 10.3366/E1750224108000378

After Alice: Alice and the Dry Tail

Dorothea Olkowski   University of Colorado

Abstract

According to Gilles Deleuze, the underground world of *Alice in Wonderland* has been strongly associated with animality and embodiment. Thus the need for Alice's eventual climb to the surface and her discovery that everything linguistic happens at that border. Yet, strangely, in spite of the claim that Alice disavows false depth and returns to the surface, it seems that it is precisely in the depths that she finally wakes from her sleepy, stupified surface state and investigates the deep structures, the rules of logic. In this investigation, Alice questions many formal structures, such as causality, identity, reference and the rules of replacement. She discovers that Wonderland does not generate consequential conduct; in fact, it generates no conduct whatsoever! In other words, when it comes to consequences, Wonderland may not be all that wonderful. Yet, we do not live in Wonderland and therefore, our actions have consequences. The question this poses is, why organise language so as to escape causal relations and why choose the little girl as emblematic of this organisation?

Keywords: Alice in Wonderland, surface, deep structure, linguistics, logic, causality, little girl.

The Long Fall

On a very hot day, raised out of her sleepy state by the astonishing sight of a rabbit removing a watch from the pocket of the waistcoat it was *wearing*, a little girl named Alice runs after the creature. She races across a field and, without hesitation, follows it down a large rabbit-hole hidden under a hedge. She falls from the surface of the earth into the depths, seemingly endlessly, into the rabbit's hole, ' "Down, down, down. Would the fall never come to an end?" '[1] The fall takes so long that Alice starts to get sleepy again and she shakes herself out of it, perhaps, not surprisingly, by talking to herself, and perhaps, somewhat surprisingly, by beginning to engage with the conventions of logic: Does 'All A are B' convert, she asks, to 'All B are A' as in the questions, 'Do cats eat bats?' and 'Do bats eat cats?' (Carroll 1974: 16). But because she is unable to provide a solid empirical answer for herself regarding the dietary habits of the creatures in question, she forgets about this problem the moment she finally lands upon a heap of dry leaves. However, on her feet once again, but now deep underground, she begins exploring this place in which she finds herself, and she continues articulating her discoveries in terms of logical rules.

Perhaps this is startling, for the underground world has been strongly associated with animality and embodiment. Only animals, it has been said, are deep, and depth is no compliment. 'The entire first half of Alice still seeks the secret of events... in the depths of the earth, in dugout shafts and holes which plunge beneath, and in the mixture of bodies which interpenetrate and coexist' (Deleuze 1990: 9 [19]).[2] This leads, we are told, to Alice's eventual climb to the surface and her disavowal of false depth, her discovery that everything linguistic happens at that border. Yet, strangely, in spite of the claim (coming from Gilles Deleuze), that Alice disavows false depth and returns to the surface, it seems that it is precisely in the depths that she finally wakes from her sleepy, stupefied surface state and investigates the deep structures, the rules of logic. In this investigation, Alice questions many formal structures, such as causality, identity, reference and the rules of replacement, and as we shall see, she discovers that as wonderful as unleashing these formal structures might be, nevertheless Wonderland does not generate consequential conduct. In fact it, generates no conduct whatsoever! In other words, when it comes to consequences, Wonderland may not be all that wonderful.

Finding herself in a long hallway of locked doors and spotting a tiny gold key on a table, Alice again talks to herself, this time addressing herself with a disjunctive proposition. *Either* the locks are too large *or* the key she finds is too small to open any of the doors in the great hall. This is followed by a set of hypotheticals. *If* eating the little cake she finds under the table makes her larger, *then* she can reach the key that she left on the table. However, *if* it makes her smaller, *then* she can creep under the door leading into the lovely garden. Having begun her musings with these disjunctive propositions, Alice alerts the reader to the possibility of putting into play the so-called 'rules of replacement:' rules governing logically equivalent expressions which permit an inference from any statement that results from replacing any component of that statement with a logically equivalent statement (Copi and Cohen 1994: 387–8).[3]

Therefore, given any hypothetical statement, 'if p, then q,' which consists of a relation between two propositions, 'p,' and 'q,' and which invokes a causal relation between 'p' and 'q,' the statement can be reformulated using the rule of material implication to arrive at its logical equivalent, 'not p or q,' (Devlin 1994: 48).[4] In this way, Alice can be said to create a series of disjunctive terms, beginning with, '*either* the locks are too large *or* the key she finds is too small to open any of the doors in the great hall.' From there we proceed to the next set of disjunctions in the series. *Either* it is not the case that the bottle named 'DRINK ME' will make her smaller *or* she can go through the little door. So we are lead to the discovery, with Alice, that propositions that might have been stated as linear and causal hypotheticals can be transformed into a series of disjunctions bearing no causal relation to one another. This is the reason why anything is possible. By evading causality, one may evade consequences. Evading consequences implies that actions are mere events with no before and no after, no causes and no effects, no actors and no one or no thing responsible. In other words, Alice discovers a world without good sense.

Of course, even after opening our and her eyes to the replacement of the series of causal relations that would have allowed her to proceed in the manner of good sense, Alice remains cognisant of causality. In other words, using good sense, the sense of temporal or causal relations, she remains cognisant of the arrow of time, and thus constitutes the relation between what is most differentiated (poison, which might be the contents of the bottle named DRINK ME) and so fixed in the past, and what is less differentiated and oriented as the future (the disagreeable results of drinking poison) (Deleuze 1990: 75 [93]). She does this with the aid of memory. Alice remembers that a red-hot poker will burn you if you hold it too long, that cutting one's finger very deeply with a knife usually results in bleeding, and that drinking from a bottle marked 'poison' will indeed have disagreeable results (Carroll 1974: 18–9). But it must be stressed that these relations are all things she merely remembers and that her current adventures continue along a disjointed trajectory. In this sense, she is correct, as she puts it, to 'think that very few things indeed were really impossible,' at least while she is underground (Carroll 1974: 18). Drinking from the bottle named 'DRINK ME,' she shrinks to a mere 10 inches, but having left the key on the table, she is still unable to get through the door into the lovely garden. (*Either* she will not shrink any further *or* she will go out like the flame of a candle.) Upon finding a very small cake named 'EAT ME' under the table, she states the following: *Either* it is not the case that eating the cake will make her larger *or* she can reach the key. And, *either* it is *not* the case that the cake will make her smaller *or* she can creep under the door (Carroll 1974: 20).

It seems that it is the power of disjunction, as much as, if not more than, the things she drinks and eats that convince Alice, at least at this point, that it would be dull and stupid for life to go on in the common way. Yet memory supplies her with the recollection of little children, who suffered burns, had been eaten by beasts, or suffered other disagreeable outcomes because they did not remember the simple rules about these sorts of things. However, insofar as eating the cake is disjoined from its effects, then it cannot provide Alice with any causal information that she might apply to drinking from the bottle. Disjunction convinces Alice that as long as the bottle is not named 'poison' (something she merely remembers) she need not concern herself with the arrow of time. Alas. For when she drinks from the bottle, tasting as it does of a very nice concoction of flavors, not only does Alice grow so large that she can barely even see her own feet, but more: she begins talking what she refers to as nonsense, carrying on speaking to herself about her feet as if they were not part of her and might walk off in a different direction if she is not kind to them, so that her feet need to be convinced not to do this. It seems that her ability to proceed according to disjunctive statements leads her to what logicians call, the 'vicious circle principle,' which is that 'no entity can be defined in terms of a totality of which it is itself a possible member' (Tiles 1991: 72).[5] In other words, if a name is taken to be a label for an empirically given object, it is a logically proper name with reference but no sense. If it is a descriptive expression, it identifies an object in terms of its relations to other objects or as constructed out of previously given objects. The logical problem here is that no entity can be constructed out of itself and no verbal expression can be defined in terms of itself (Tiles 1991: 79–81).[6] Yet this is precisely what Alice tries to do. And so, speaking to herself concerning her feet has taken her to the point of speaking nonsense. Her problem is that insofar as, 'an element cannot be part of the sub-sets which it determines' (for example, Alice and her feet), nor a part of the set whose existence it presupposes (thus, her feet and Alice), logically, she is engaged in a vicious circle. Either way, she is not making sense! (Deleuze 1990: 69 [86]).

Not only does Alice begin speaking nonsense but additionally, while fanning herself with a fan dropped by the White Rabbit whom she frightens (as she is now 9 feet high), Alice begins asking questions about her own identity: 'Was I the same as when I got up this morning? I almost think I can remember feeling a little different. But if I'm not the same, the next question is, Who in the world am I?' (Carroll 1974: 24). As we can see, this is not just pretend angst. Poor Alice has changed so much that she can no longer recite her multiplication tables, nor can she remember geography or recite a short verse correctly. In other words, the past is not carrying into the present; good sense is not functioning, and this is having an effect on her identity. So it may be that having forgone good sense, Alice is now faced with the loss of common sense as well, if common sense is in fact what 'subsumes under itself the various faculties of the soul, or the differentiated organs of the body, and brings them to bear upon a unity which is capable of saying "I"' (Deleuze 1990: 78 [96]). 'Let me think,' she asks herself, 'was I the same when I got up this morning? I almost think I can remember feeling a little different. But if I'm not the same, the next question is, "Who in the world am I?"' (Carroll 1974: 24). And she resolves not to return above ground until her identity is resolved to her satisfaction. Contemporary philosophers often take such a turn of events to be a positive development. The disappearance of the author or of the self is celebrated as an encouraging step away from the concept of a centered, egoistic subject. But for Alice, it could have serious consequences: she could in fact go out like a flame! Fortunately, just before shrinking completely out of sight, Alice realises that there is a causal relation between fanning herself and growing small again and she stops fanning just in time.

A Dry Tail

Good sense at least partially restored, Alice nonetheless falls into the pool of tears that she, herself has cried. Suddenly and inexplicably surrounded by strange creatures (a Duck and a Dodo, a Lory and an Eaglet, a Mouse and others), who simply appear and fall into the water, then follow her to shore, Alice is once again faced with logical and linguistic problems.[7] In particular, the Mouse has trouble with the *sense* of words. The Mouse tells the driest story it knows in order to dry off the company who are all wet from falling into the pool of tears, and when it offers to tell a long *tale*, Alice can only imagine a long *tail* (Carroll 1974: 30–6). The problem that interferes with communication here seems to be related to the question of distinguishing sense and reference. Sense and reference have been defined, most notably, by the philosopher, Gottlob Frege. For Frege, a sign or a name represents a proper name which must have a definite object as its reference. Moreover, although a definite sense corresponds to the sign, certain signs (the extinct Dodo) have sense yet no reference. The reference of a sign is an object able to be perceived by the senses (the long tale that we hear or the long tail that we see) of which we may form an internal image, an idea, arising from memories of sense impressions (Frege 1952: 57–9). What *this* means is that sense does not assure that there is a reference and therefore, the same sense is not always connected with the same idea (Frege 1952: 59).

The Mouse and Alice connect different ideas to the name *dry*. Alice wants to dry off because she is wet, cold and shivering. The Mouse wants to tell a dry story: thus the importance of reference. The reference of tale, tail or dry is an object which we designate, but the idea is wholly subjective (to dry off or to tell a dry tale) (Frege 1952: 60). 'In between lies the sense, which is indeed no longer subjective like the idea, but is yet not the object itself' (Frege 1952: 60). 'A proper name (word, sign, sign combination, expression) expresses its sense, stands for or designates its reference. By means of a sign we express its sense and designate its reference' (Frege 1952: 61). And, just like the Duck, who demands to know what 'it' means when the mouse dryly relates that 'Stigand, the patriotic archbishop of Canterbury, found it advisable,' Frege also finds that when we say something we presuppose a reference and preferably, something with a proper name (Carroll 1974: 30; Frege 1952: 61). For the Duck, *it* refers to a frog or a worm that the Duck has actually found (and not simply thought about) and so *it* must have both a sense and a reference in order for saying *it* to matter to us at all. We want the proper name to have a reference, Frege states, because of our concern with truth value. Poems and stories that convey only sense and feeling through their images do not lend themselves to truth. Thus the dry tale is not meant to delight but to convey something true. Truth value is identified with reference and all true sentences must have the referent 'true' and all false sentences have the referent 'false.' This allows the Duck to replace frog or worm with the name *it*, but still seems to undermine the Mouse, who wished to tell a dry story, a story with truth value (Frege 1952: 64–5). For the Mouse's *it* may have sense, yet it appears to be without reference.

And so, one might argue that Alice is beginning to recognise the limits of undoing causality and the problems associated with sense and reference, and it is this that eventually sends her fleeing back to the surface. When the White Rabbit abruptly orders her to find his gloves and fan, taking her to be the maid (she is a girl after all), Alice also finds a bottle named 'DRINK ME.' She seems to take this name to be an imperative, even though this time, she *knows*, as she puts it, that something interesting (as she also puts it), will happen each time she eats or drinks anything (Carroll 1974: 38). She does not just remember that there have been causal relations between eating and drinking and something interesting in the past, but she claims to *know* that causal relations are operating in her present as well. Moreover, Alice's identity is not the only one in question. Little pebbles are thrown at her, in an unsuccessful effort to kill her or drive her out, as she sits despondently in the White Rabbit's house where she has gone to fetch the gloves and fan. As they hit her, the pebbles turn into little cakes; fortunately, she anticipates that by eating them, she will shrink again (Carroll 1974: 43). Indeed, this is exactly what happens. Good sense seems to be once again operating even though Alice's identity remains uncertain and problematic. Thus the question 'Who are you?' when posed by the hookah smoking Caterpillar is more than appropriate, even though, as the story makes clear, 'This was not an encouraging opening for a conversation' (Carroll 1974: 47). Alice cannot explain *herself* but the Caterpillar does not understand this at all and continues to speak to Alice with some contempt, prodding her eventually to try to recite a verse correctly, at which, of course, she completely fails, offering instead, an irreverent parody of the original, in which the old and corpulent father threatens to kick the inquisitive son down the stairs, a story that is 'wrong from beginning to end' (Carroll 1974: 54).

It is in light of such stories, Gilles Deleuze asserts, that Lewis Carroll detests boys in general. The male baby in Alice turns into a pig. Boys, it seems, are associated with animality, with organs, with the objects of smell, taste and touch that are perceived, imagined or remembered. And boys are associated with the self that breathes, sleeps and walks following the laws of a determined system (Deleuze 1990: 78 [96]). In *Silvie and Bruno*, Deleuze claims, the little boy is the inventive thinker only by becoming a little girl, passing from reality to dream, from bodies to the incorporeal, bringing to language becoming and its paradoxes (Deleuze 1990: 10–1 [20]). By contrast, the little girl is said to eagerly abandon good-sense and common-sense, to undo causality and identity, and this it is implied is to be something laudable. Indeed, it ends (in Deleuze) with the girl or the woman being characterised as the molecular becoming of the molar boy or man. Yet Alice does not necessarily associate boys with animality and with the senses. She is concerned when the baby is nearly hit in nose by the shower of pans, plates and dishes thrown by the cook. ' "Oh please mind what you're doing!" cried Alice in an agony of terror. "Oh, there goes his precious nose;" as an unusually large saucepan flew close by it, and very nearly carried it off' (Carroll 1974: 58). Certainly the Duchess seems to abuse the little boy, violently shaking and tossing him and recommending (in her so-called lullaby) speaking roughly and beating him! But then, she speaks roughly to Alice as well, ordering the cook to chop off her head; and the cook is throwing pans at the Duchess, Alice and the baby! (Carroll 1974: 59–60). The Duchess finally throws the child at Alice who reflects that, 'If I don't take this child away with me, ... they're sure to kill it in a day or two: wouldn't it be murder to leave it behind?' (Carroll 1974: 60). And, upon hearing the baby grunt, she looks at it anxiously while 'the poor little thing sobbed again' (Carroll 1974: 61). It is only when it finally transforms completely into what she calls a rather handsome pig that she lets it go, thinking about other children she knows who might also be pigs. And such transformations, as we have seen, are entirely possible in a world of disjunction, where causal chains have been torn apart. Perhaps it is the Cheshire Cat who provides the best explanation of what is going on, claiming that everyone there is mad, including itself. And as it too invokes the vicious circle principle, appearing and vanishing so that only its grin remains: how can the grin be defined as belonging to, as part of the cat? If it does belong to the cat, then it cannot be distinguished from the cat. To do so, might not be madness, but it is certainly nonsense.

Tea and No Sympathy

Reaching the Mad Hatter's, Alice is again met with considerable rudeness. She is offered wine when there is none. She is told that she needs a haircut. She is told she is stupid and generally treated rudely. She is given a riddle to guess, but it has no answer. She is tricked into making logical errors. Hoping to guess the answer to the riddle, she is asked ' "Do you think that you can find out the answer to it?"..... "Exactly so," said Alice. "Then you should say what you mean" .... "I do," Alice hastily replied – "at least I mean what I say – that's the same thing, you know"' (Carroll 1974: 67). Of course, it's not the same thing. Of course, the problem still involves the relation between sense and reference. Alice *means* that she can solve the riddle, but also she *says* that she means that she can solve the riddle. For her, there are two different references, so in fact, it's not the same thing. She must sort this out for herself so as not to be caught in a logical error, such as that of declaring that the referent of the name 'Time' is a 'he' and that the sense of the expression 'killing time' can result in a murder and a permanent 6 o'clock, which just happens to be tea-time (Carroll 1974: 70).

In his analysis of the significance of sentences, Bertrand Russell argues that there are three sorts of sentence, those that are true, those that are false, and those that are nonsensical (Russell 1940: 172). The latter are clearly not true but also, they are not false; when a sentence is nonsense, or meaningless as Russell calls it, then so is its negation. Paradox arises from sentences that seem to signify something but really do not. Still it is not clear how to distinguish sentences that signify something and those that do not. Significance, according to Russell, must be propositional, able to be true or false (Russell 1940: 175). This, in turn, relies on perceptual experiences that can be imagined or that actually occur, making us use a phrase as an assertion. The phrase uttered during tea by the Dormouse, 'They were learning to draw ... everything that begins with an M –' can be significant if it is true (Carroll 1974: 74). However, what is *expressed* must be distinguished from what makes a statement true. Expression is a state of mind, a belief or even a desire that others should have this belief (Russell 1940: 175). For Alice, since the drawing lesson is supposed to be taking place at the bottom of a treacle-well, this claim strains her credulity; she does not believe it. Assertion, however, is not the same as expression. One does not assert the belief that is being expressed, rather one asserts that the *object* of the belief is true or false. Thus, asserting that three little girls are sitting in the bottom of a treacle well learning to draw things that begin with the letter M (things such as mouse-traps, moon, memory and *muchness*) truly confuses Alice! No wonder she declares, 'Its the stupidest tea-party I ever was at in all my life!' (Carroll 1974: 75). Lacking significance, the Dormouse's story is pure nonsense. That Alice's credulity is challenged and that she slips away is evidence that her identity is less in question, even if she does not yet notice this.

The order of language just set out is severely questioned by Deleuze. Addressing Russell's assertion that denotation, manifestation (the statement of beliefs or desires), and signification are the three accepted relations holding for a proposition, Deleuze brings the proposition back to nonsense (Russell 1940: 171).[8] That is, manifestation is precisely the relation that Alice comes to expect and when it does not occur; what she hears *she* takes for nonsense. At the tea party, she expects that beliefs or desires are causal inferences that correspond to the proposition (Deleuze 1990: 13 [23]). Following Russell, Deleuze states that desire is an inference between the internal causality of an image and the existence of an object or state of affairs. Belief is also an inference; it is the anticipation of an object or state of affairs produced by external causality (Deleuze 1990:13 [23]). Manifestation, the statement of beliefs or desires, always involves the 'I,' so that, for example, what Alice believes – her belief – grounds her judgment regarding denotation. Denotation is the relation of the proposition to an external state of affairs. Alice has a hard time believing the Dormouse's story that three little girls are living in a treacle-well. 'True,' would signify that the denotation is fulfilled by a particular state of affairs; 'false' signifies that the denotation is not fulfilled. But Deleuze reads this differently from Russell. Russell, we noted above, demands that significance be propositional (meaning true or false) and this, in turn, relies on perceptual experiences, something Deleuze clearly rejects. Referring not to significance but to signification, Deleuze never mentions perception or experience. Instead, he states that signification is the relation of a word to universal or general concepts; it involves good sense (Deleuze 1990: 14 [24]). It seems that Deleuze departs from Russell and returns here to the same ideas as those asserted by Frege who, we have noted, states that sense does not assure that there is a reference, thus doing away with the necessity of empirical verification (Frege 1952: 59). Since the sense is no longer subjective like the idea, but is also not the object, it must be something else (Frege 1952: 60). Sense is, it seems, a fourth dimension. Specifically, as Frege has stated, a proper name (word, sign, sign combination, expression) *expresses* its sense and stands for or designates its reference.

To make sense of sense, Frege asks that we consider a sentence and not merely proper names. Sentences contain thoughts, that is, objective content, something capable of being the common property of several thinkers (Frege 1952: 62). This objective content is the sense of the sentence, but it seems possible that sentences may have sense but no reference at all! 'The Dodo fell into the pool of tears,' seems to be one such sentence. And, if one wanted to go no further than this thought, *there would be no need to assign a reference*. The thought remains the same whether 'Dodo' has a reference or not. Truth forces us to abandon certain affects, particularly those such as aesthetic delight (Frege 1952: 63). But truth also forces language away from the 'idea' or the 'Idea' and back to the perceptual, the phenomenological. Still, if we are not concerned about truth, we need not be concerned about reference. Thus we can understand why, strictly speaking, if we are not concerned about reference, sense does not exist outside of the proposition that expresses it (Deleuze 1990: 21 [33]). Sense is therefore a logical attribute, but one that does not and is not compelled to describe a physical state of affairs; it does not require a referent; it is the event that is *no longer causally linked* to what came before or what comes after: 'The event belongs essentially to language' (Deleuze 1990: 22 [34]). With this, Deleuze pushes a bit, revising the arguments of the logicians: 'It seems difficult to say... that the fantastic work [of Lewis Carroll] presents simply the traps and difficulties into which we fall when we do not observe the rules and laws formulated by the logical work' (Deleuze 1990: 22 [34]). Admittedly, Carroll's work is about signification, implication and conclusions, but to what end? Is it, as Deleuze argues, in order to introduce paradoxes that signification does not resolve and even creates, or is it to raise other still unanswered question?

Molecular Becoming, The Making of a Philosopher

Escaping the tea party through a door that she notices in a tree, Alice finds herself back in the long hall, a curious return. Spying the little golden key on the glass table, she recalls her previous experience and puts into play her causal knowledge. First she takes the key and unlocks the garden door, then she nibbles carefully a bit of the mushroom which she had saved! Now only a foot high, she can at last walk through the door and go into the beautiful garden with its bright flower-beds and cool fountains (Carroll 1974: 76). There she finds gardeners who are nothing but playing cards (two, five and seven of hearts are painting the white flowers red), as well as soldiers, courtiers, kings and queens, and finally 'THE KING AND QUEEN OF HEARTS' (Carroll 1974: 78). Although she is very small, Alice does realise, 'they're only a pack of cards, after all. I needn't be afraid of them' (Carroll 1974: 78). And even when the Queen, in a fury, screams, 'Off with her head!,' meaning Alice's head, nothing unfortunate happens. In Wonderland, where words do not signify and causality is disjoined, such statements have no consequences. Invited to play a very odd sort of croquet with playing cards for wires, flamingos for mallets and hedgehogs for balls, Alice remains concerned about the Queen's constant demand for beheadings and she notices that no one plays fairly, that the game has no rules, and that it is very confusing with everything alive and moving all the time. Moreover, during the entire game, the Queen never stops quarrelling with the players, till Alice feels quite frightened again. The Duchess appears (released from prison where she was placed for boxing the Queen's ears). Informing Alice that, 'Everything's got a moral, if only you can find it,' she squeezes herself up unpleasantly close to Alice, putting her sharp chin on the little girl's shoulder (Carroll 1974: 86). And the Duchess does have a *moral* for everything; but in Wonderland its no surprise that the moral has nothing to do with the event for which it is supposed to be the moral! When Alice timidly states that the game is going better, the Duchess responds that the moral of that is 'tis love, 'tis love that makes the world go round!' (Carroll 1974: 87).

With almost all the players in prison for various faults, Alice is taken by the Queen for one final adventure, the Mock Turtle's story. There she listens to the Mock Turtle's sad tale, which is that once he had been a *real* turtle who had studied a wild list of courses from the Master turtle called 'Tortoise' (because he taught them) (Carroll 1974: 92). They teach her to dance the lobster quadrille and although Alice is rather bored by much of this, she struggles to be polite. They do not notice the extreme nonsense of their own stories, school subjects such as 'the different branches of Arithmetic – Ambition, Distraction, Uglification, and Derision' as well as '– Mystery, ancient and modern, with Seaography; then Drawling –' (Carroll 1974: 94, 95). But when Alice tells them her own story, they readily agree that her recollection of the poem, *'Father William'* is seriously flawed, uncommon nonsense. Alice 'sat down with her face in her hands and wondered if anything would *ever* happen in a natural way again' (Carroll 1974: 102).

The final episode erupts when the Gryphon hears the call to come to the trial of the Knave of Hearts, accused of stealing tarts which sit on the table in front of all in the courtroom. At the trial, Alice is pleased to be able to identify the judge and the jury, but forgets her manners and cries out that the jurors are stupid because they must write down even their names, lest they forget them. Problems with identity are spread far and wide. During the trial Alice begins to grow again, physically, and seeing the tarts makes her feel quite hungry. It is as if embodiment and growth are having an effect. She also grows impatient with the illogicality of the court. The judge (who is the King) does not seem to be able to discern what is and what is not evidence and commands the jurors to write down nearly everything said, no matter how foolish. When witnesses are called, the King threatens to execute them if they act nervous or if they cannot remember. Of course, given that causality has been abandoned, it would be surprising if any witness could remember anything. When an unsigned letter is introduced as evidence, the King takes its lack of signature as evidence that the Knave must be guilty or he would have signed it. And, in spite of the fact that the letter contains no names, no references whatsoever, the King believes it points in the direction of the Knave's guilt.

As Alice begins to grow, she also grows up. When the King announces, 'Rule Forty-two, *All persons more than a mile high to leave the court,'* and proclaims it to be the oldest rule in the book, Alice is quick to assert that she is not a mile high and that anyway, if it were the oldest rule it would be Number One (Carroll 1974: 114). Nor is she afraid of stating that there's not an atom of meaning in the anonymous letter read to the courts. When, following the well established convention of Wonderland, the Queen calls for the sentence before the verdict, Alice loudly objects: 'Stuff and nonsense!' she scoffs, 'The idea of having the sentence first!' (Carroll 1974: 119). Enraged, the Queen orders Alice to hold her tongue and when Alice refuses, the Queen commands, 'Off with her head!' which only incites Alice to proclaim the lot of them to be nothing but a pack of cards (Carroll 1974: 119). And when the cards rise up and attack her, she beats them off and then finds herself once again lying on the bank with her sister, waking as if from a dream.

Feminist philosophers have noted the unusual role that Alice in particular and the little girl in general play in Deleuze's work. Catherine Driscoll asserts that, 'Deleuze frequently aligns Alice with becoming, and through Alice insists that becoming is a paradox defined as "the affirmation of both senses or directions at the same time.". Becoming always suggests a movement across time, indeed becoming as transformative process is not necessarily opposed to standard models of development: there is a quite commonsensical sense in which one might be becoming mad, becoming tall or becoming woman. But becoming for Deleuze is strictly opposed to any linear conception of time' (Driscoll 2000). Rosi Braidotti adds that Deleuze complains that 'feminists refuse to dissolve the subject "woman" into a series of transformative processes that pertain to a generalized and "postgender" becoming,' and that although politically correct, this is conceptually mistaken (Braidotti 1994: 116). Clearly, Deleuze and Félix Guattari recognise this. Below Oedipus, for example, they claim to discover a molecular unconscious; beneath the stable forms, functionalism; under familialism, polymorphous perversity (Deleuze and Guattari 1987: 283–96). And so, beneath woman or even man, the little girl, Alice in Wonderland, releases becoming from the constraints of reference, signification, identity and causation, making it possible to take apart whatever has been joined together and to reverse direction and deny the arrow of time. Underlying all this is the distinction between the molecular and the molar, the microphysical and the statistical.

In the most formal, mathematical sense of the term, the molecular refers to Avogadro's number, the number of atoms needed such that the number of grams of a substance equals the atomic mass of the substance. An Avogadro's number of substance is called a mole (Schneider and Sagan 2005: xi).[9] Avogadro's hypothesis was key to solving many problems in the chemical sciences in the 1800s. For chemistry, molecules and moles are a matter of physical relations, ascertaining that equal volumes of gases with the same pressure and temperature contain the same number of molecules. By analogy, these terms reveal several possibilities: first that 'the machine taken in its structural unity, the living taken in its specific and even personal unity, are mass phenomena or *molar aggregates*... merely two paths in the same statistical direction' (Deleuze and Guattari 1983: 286). From the point of view of molar or statistical aggregates in physical relations, there is no difference between machine and life; *molar machines* may be social machines, technical machines, or organic machines. As such, they may be language machines. And what of the molecular? All becomings are molecular. So the becoming-woman and becoming-child do not resemble the woman or the child, which are the molar forms arising with language that signifies and refers, enacts causality and identity (good sense and common sense).

But what is quite *curious* is that the woman has to become-woman in order for the man to become-woman. In writing, atoms of woman-hood, particles sweep across the social field and contaminate even men! (Deleuze and Guattari 1987: 276). Society steals the girl's becoming and imposes a history on her, makes her an object of desire, an example and a trap. Is the entire history of men's writing then nothing more than an escape from this trap, an escape from consequences and the arrow of time (Deleuze and Guattari 1987: 276)? Carroll points to the idea that, in Wonderland, where causality and reference no longer reign, anything is possible. Causal links of any kind are dissolved. But in fact what occurs is that *nothing happens*. A tea party is eternal. The Queen orders beheadings all day long and not a single one occurs. A trial is seemingly held but no evidence is gathered. And in any case, if something does happen, it's a simple matter to undo it; the pig could just as well turn back into a baby. By implication, therefore, no one is responsible for anything because nothing takes place and, in any case, lacking reference, all is Idea, nothing but Idea. This is, Deleuze and Guattari state, the only way to get outside of dualisms, by producing an Idea, the universal girl, the key to all becoming.

Yet, we do not live in Wonderland and therefore, our actions have consequences. That Deleuze and Guattari choose the little girl as the origin of all becomings evinces a fundamental binarism at the heart of their philosophy. Molecules are neither male nor female; such a deter-mination is purely molar. Why choose girls, unless their molar existence is already in question? Why organise language so as to escape causal relations, unless to eliminate the possibility of that a little girl might grow up? Let us not forget Alice's *older sister*, 'sitting just as she left her, leaning her head on her hand, watching the setting sun, and thinking of little Alice and all her wonderful Adventures' (Carroll 1974: 120). Her surface world comes alive with all the creatures of Alice's adventures, but the older sister knows that these creatures and events are versions of the reality around her. Carroll calls it 'dull reality,' but describes something quite different. He describes grass rustling in the wind, a pool rippling to the wave of reeds, tinkling sheep-bells, the shepherd-boy's voice, the confused clamor of the busy farm-yard. Truly, are these dull realities or are they part of the beauty and joy of life? And Alice? Through all her years, she would keep the simple and loving heart of her childhood, gathering other children about her to tell them her tales. She would feel their sorrows and find pleasure in their simple joys. But Carroll leaves out one thing. He forgets to say that Alice will also understand the limits of language and logic, the limits of a limitless world of possibilities, a world without causality and identity, without the arrow of time, without signification or reference. And in understanding this, Alice will be not just a woman with a simple and pure heart but a woman who understands: a thinker... a philosopher.

References

Braidotti, Rosi (1994) *Nomadic Subjects: Embodiment and Sexual Difference in Contemporary Feminist Theory*, New York: Columbia University Press.

Carroll, Lewis (1974) *The Philosopher's Alice in Wonderland and Through the Looking-Glass*, introduction and notes by Peter Heath, New York: St. Martin's Press.

Copi, Irving M. and Carl Cohen (1994) *Introduction to Logic*, New York: MacMillan.

Deleuze, Gilles (1969) *Logique du Sens*, Paris: Les Editions de Minuit.

Deleuze, Gilles (1990) *The Logic of Sense*, trans. Mark Lester, with Charles Stivale; Constantin V. Boundas ed. New York: Columbia University Press.

Deleuze, Gilles and Félix Guattari (1983) *Anti-Oedipus*, trans. Robert Hurley, Mark Seem, and Helen R. Lane, Minneapolis: University of Minnesota Press. [Originally published as *Anti-Oedipe*, Paris: Les Editions de Minuit, 1972.]

Devlin, Keith (1994) *Mathematics: The Science of Patterns*, New York: Scientific American Library.

Driscoll, Catherine (2000) 'The Little Girl, Deleuze and Guattari', in Gary Genosko (ed.), *Critical Assessments of Leading Philosophers*, Vol. 3, London and New York: Routledge. [Reprinted from Antithesis, 8.2, 1997.]

Frege, Gottlob (1952) 'On Sense and Reference', in *Translations from the Philosophical Writings of Gottlob Frege*, ed. Peter Geach and Max Black, Oxford: Basil Blackwell.

Russell, Bertrand (1940) *An Inquiry Into Meaning and Truth*, London: Allen and Unwin.

Tiles, Mary (1991) *Mathematics and the Image of Reason*, London and New York: Routledge Press.

Schneider, Eric D. and Dorian Sagan (2005) *Into the Cool: Energy Flow, Thermodynamics and Life*, Chicago: University of Chicago Press.

Notes

1. I am using Lewis Carroll (1974), *The Philosopher's Alice in Wonderland and Through the Looking-Glass*, Introduction and notes by Peter Heath, 15. This edition is subtitled 'The Thinking Man's Guide to a Misunderstood Nursery Classic,' but I have found little in the notes to enlighten a thinking *woman*.
2. References are to the English version with the French original (1969) in [ ].
3. 'In any truth functional compound statement, if a component statement in it is replaced by another statement having the same truth value, the truth value of the compound statement will remain unchanged' (Copi and Cohen 1994: 387–88).
4. If p then q = (not p) or q.
5. Bertrand Russell's solution to this was to create a hierarchy of types of objects and a corresponding hierarchy of concepts so that no individual is a member of its own class.
6. The position is atomist in that it accords reality only to empirical objects and their relations, not to structure (Tiles 1991: 85).
7. As we have seen, no causal explanation for their sudden appearance is necessary.
8. Russell argues that assertions have a subjective side and an objective side. The subjective side is found in the expression of the speaker's beliefs or desires. The objective side is the assertion's intention to indicate an object. Russell identifies the significance of a sentence with what it expresses. True and false sentences may be equally significant but in order for a string of words not to be just nonsense, it must express the beliefs or desires of the speaker. Additionally, if the string of words is nonsense, it cannot have an effect on a hearer.
9. They refer here to the poet, Joseph Brodsky, who wrote that humans are closer to the big bang than to Rome (Schneider and Sagan 2005: xi).

DOI: 10.3366/E175022410800038X

Phallocentrism in Bergson: Life and Matter

Rebecca Hill   Royal Melbourne Institute of Technology

Abstract

Henri Bergson's philosophy presents the relationship between life and matter in both dualistic and monistic terms. Life is duration, a rhythm of incalculable novelty that approaches pure creative activity. In stark contrast, matter is identified with the determinism of homogeneous space. After *Time and Free Will*, Bergson concedes some share of duration to matter. In this context, his dualism can be understood as a methodological step towards the articulation of a monistic metaphysics of duration. This article suggests that the distinction between life and matter is also motivated by an unconscious imperative to establish a sexed hierarchy. Bergson repeatedly presents life as seminal, while matter is figured in terms of passivity.

Keywords: Bergson, sexed hierarchy, matter, life, duration, monism, dualism, extension.

In Henri Bergson's open system, life is conceived as duration. Famously, the creative evolution of life cannot be reduced to numerical calculation or adequately symbolised in any diagram. It is a flow of heterogeneous and continuous becoming that radically exceeds the present[1] (Bergson 1983: 2–4/496–8). In stark contrast, matter is defined as 'a present which is always beginning again' (1981: 139/281). For Bergson, each of matter's presents is 'practically equivalent' to the next one, which means in theory that it is possible to calculate a moment of the material world from its previous moment (1981: 247–8/376–7). In this sense matter is almost indistinguishable from the pure intelligibility of homogeneous space.

Bergson construes the relationship between life and matter in both dualistic and monistic terms. Gilles Deleuze has argued that Bergson's use of dualism is methodological. Bergson dichotomises in order to recover real duration from the disfiguring medium of homogeneous space, which occludes becoming by submitting it to calculability (Deleuze 1988: 29). After disentangling purely temporal living phenomena from space, Bergson is able to reintegrate life and matter into an evolving whole in which the difference between the creative speeds of life and the almost determined rhythm of matter is a difference in temporal tension (Deleuze 1988: 29). While I am in partial agreement with Deleuze's suggestion that Bergson's predilection for dualism is a provisional step in the establishment of a monistic metaphysics, I claim that the tendency to dichotomise is more than a methodological manoeuvre. Bergson's commitment to dualism can be read as symptomatic of a disavowal of a sexed hierarchy at the very heart of his open system. Further, I suggest that Bergson's celebrated monistic integration of the divergent tendencies of life and matter maintains this sexed hierarchy.

The sexuation of Bergson's thought is betrayed in his use of metaphor and image. This is particularly significant because in Bergson images and metaphors are privileged in his method. For Bergson, language is spatial in essence, which means that he cannot present the intuition of duration as such. Therefore precise use of image and metaphor is often a better way to convey the mobility of real time because they can 'suggest' the intuition of duration in a 'direct vision' (Bergson 1992: 43/1285).

I. Dualism as Method and Disavowed Masculinism

Bergson's use of dualism is directly related to his critique of the failure of the western tradition to trace the impact of the demands of practical life upon human knowledge. Before anything else, all forms of life are obliged to obtain food and shelter and seek protection from threats of injury and death. Bergson calls this the law of 'attention to life' (*l'attention à la vie*) (1981: 173/ 312).

According to Bergson, human beings have evolved a highly motivated form of knowledge to fulfil their bodily needs: intellection. The intellect is at home working with inert objects. When confronted with mobile and enduring phenomena, human intellectual representation dissolves the passage of time and mobility into static symbols such as points, axes, and lines sketched onto a grid of space. For Bergson spatialisation stems from the vital tendency to action that precedes the systematic formulations of the Greeks. He calls it, 'a latent geometry, immanent to our idea of space, which is the main spring (*le grand ressort*) of our intellect and the cause of its working' (1983: 211/674). In other words, the projection of homogeneous space, masquerading as an adequate measurement of time is one of the primary functions of the intellect. Indeed, for Bergson, the structure of human understanding demands the masking of duration. It enables us to delimit objects with clear and distinct outlines that are perfectly suited to facilitate our actions upon them (1983: 211/674).

Bergson's claim that spatialisation derives from a vital human tendency is Eurocentric. The intellectual procedure in which a subject isolates objects as immobile and delineates them with clear outlines in homogeneous space is alien to many Aboriginal philosophies. For example, Irene Watson, a Nunga feminist legal scholar describes Nunga ontology in these terms: 'We are not merely on and in the land, we are of it, we speak as one voice of the Creation, the voice or song law. Land and people are one voice one song' (Watson 2002: 7).

While Bergson's account of how homogeneous space obfuscates duration does not hold as a universal description of human knowledge, it is a salient description of the cover up of time in Western thought. His critique demonstrates the need in Western philosophy for a method of thinking that is capable of grasping time, the method he calls intuition. Where intellect limits its scope to the preparation of action, Bergsonian intuition extends to the whole of living reality. Real time and mobility are the primary objects of intuition. This is the context in which dualism emerges as a necessary step in the task of recovering enduring phenomena. By separating (geometrical) space from real time, Bergson articulates a philosophy of process which strives to follow the very passage of time's becoming rather than pulverising its dynamic progress into a line of equivalent points set out in a diagram.

Bergson's first major work *Time and Free Will* is strictly dualist. Matter is identified with homogeneous space and differentiated sharply from human consciousness, which is nothing but qualitative change or duration. The flow of unforeseeable novelty that characterises consciousness as duration is praised as the ground of the human self's creativity. This is not sexually neutral. Bergson writes 'the act which bears the mark of our personality is truly free, for our self alone will lay claim to its paternity' (1913/173). Here, paternity (presumably the act of insemination) is a metaphor for the very freedom of a durational act.[2]

From *Matter and Memory* onwards, Bergson concedes some share of duration to matter. This gesture allows him to reintegrate the divergent tendencies of matter and consciousness into a temporal monism. While Bergson relinquishes the stark dualism of *Time and Free Will*, he barely modifies the hierarchically sexed terms of his thinking when he shifts from a subjective focus to the more ambitious question of the life and matter relationship. In this sense Bergson's use of dualism is more than a methodological manoeuvre; it betrays a sexed hierarchy at work in his metaphysics.

II. The Force of Ascent and the Force of Descent

In *The Creative Evolution* Bergson traces a line of demarcation between the inert and the living (197–8/663). Within the whole, each inclines in the opposite direction: the movement of the inert is one of descent, whereas life is a movement of ascent. Materiality adds nothing new to the whole from moment to moment, and, in principle, its pulsations 'might be accomplished almost instantaneously, like releasing a spring.' It merely unwinds a roll ready prepared. In contrast, the ascending movement of life 'corresponds to an inner work of ripening or creating.' Becoming is life. It '*endures* essentially, and imposes its rhythm on the first [matter], which is inseparable from it' (1983: 11/503).

Bergson affirms repeatedly, insofar as inert matter is bound up in the duration of the universe, it endures. 'The universe *endures*... The systems marked off by science *endure* only because they are bound up inseparably with the rest of the universe' (1983: 11/503). He provides what is now a famous example to support his argument. If sugar is mixed in a glass of water, the observer cannot speed up or draw out the process of the sugar melting. The observer's impatience is not something thought, such as the mathematical time of the physicist; it corresponds to something lived. Waiting for the sugar to melt is not relative because the parts of time cannot be unfurled at will. It is absolute. The whole universe then, has a particular, irreducible rhythm of duration that is something like a consciousness (1983: 10/502). In other words, matter is irreducibly implicated in the duration of the living.

Intuition provides Bergson with the means to elucidate the relationship between life and matter. Characteristically, Bergson calls for the philosopher to reflect upon his own interior life.[3] In his view, this act of thinking introduces the philosopher to an intuition of the two contrary movements that make up the Whole, the movement of life and the movement of matter. To accomplish the movement of life, 'we' must seek, within 'our own' experience, 'the point we feel ourselves most intimately with our own life. It is into pure duration that we then plunge back, a duration in the past, always moving on, is swelling unceasingly with a present that is absolutely new.' (1983: 199–200/664–5) This effort is strenuous because it goes against the ingrained human habit of spatialising time. While this is an act of reflection upon the 'inner life', the temporal rhythm which the philosopher strives to discover here is not the not duration of his own life, but the duration of life itself. Bergson emphasises that the intuitive thinker can never reach this limit of pure duration, which is nothing other than freedom itself.[4]

Materiality tends in the opposite direction. From the effort of contracting as much as possible of 'our' past into the present in an undivided continuity, Bergson invites 'us' to dilate our consciousness, as far as possible.

> If the relaxation (*détente*) were complete, there would no longer be either memory or will – which amounts to saying that, in fact, we never do fall into this absolute passivity, any more than we can make ourselves absolutely free. But, in the limit, we get a glimpse (*nous entrevoyons*) of an existence made of a present which recommences unceasingly – devoid of real duration, nothing but the instantaneous which dies and is born again endlessly. (1983: 200–1/665)

Materiality *inclines* in the direction of absolute passivity but never fully dilates. If it did, it would become pure space.[5] As Bergson concedes, 'analysis resolves it into elementary vibrations, the shortest of which are of very slight duration, almost vanishing, but not nothing' (1983: 201/665). Matter and consciousness are thus defined as two opposing tendencies: the ascending movement approaching creation and freedom and the descending movement inclining toward pure repetition. In this context Bergson is able say that matter is the interruption of duration (1983: 201/665–6). Given that the entire universe endures, and materiality is irreducibly bound up in all aspects of the whole, this interruption occurs within duration, although it inclines in the inverse direction to the one articulated in the becoming of life.

For Bergson, the double effort of contraction and dilation in consciousness proceeds from the plane of experience but incites the philosopher beyond it, toward the purely qualitative and purely quantitative. Intuition is really a traversal between two extremes: unextended qualitative duration, which is absolutely continuous, and extended quantitative repetition, which lends itself to calculation and division. For Bergson:

> the intuition of duration ... brings us into contact with a whole continuity of durations which we should try to follow, either downwardly or upwardly: in both cases we can dilate ourselves indefinitely by a more and more vigorous (violent) effort, in both cases we transcend (*transcendons*) ourselves. In the first, we advance towards a duration more and more scattered (*éparpillée*), whose palpitations, more rapid than ours, dividing our simple sensation, dilute its quality into quantity: at the limit would be the pure homogeneous,

the pure repetition by which we define materiality. In advancing in the other direction, we go toward a duration which stretches, tightens, and becomes more and more intensified: at the limit would be eternity. This time not only conceptual eternity, which is an eternity of death, but an eternity of life. It would be a living, and consequently still moving eternity, where our duration would find itself like the vibrations in light, and which would be the concentration of all duration, as materiality is its dispersion (*l'éparpillement*). Between these two extreme limits moves intuition, and this movement is metaphysics itself. (1992: 187–8/1419)

We can see from the vertical movement of intuition described in this passage how Bergson reconciles the dualisms. Between the extremes of freedom and necessity, there are so many different degrees of tension, so many different degrees of extension.[6]

Bergson's temporal monism plainly privileges life over matter. On the one hand, life is celebrated for approaching freedom, and on the other hand, matter tends towards necessity. Where life has the dynamic capacity to draw upon the virtual and engender new configurations in the actual, matter is confined to the plane of the present, in which it ceaselessly makes itself from moment to moment. This hierarchical relationship is not explicitly sexed. Nonetheless, Bergson deploys traditionally phallocentric images to describe life and matter. Matter is associated with 'absolute passivity', an expression with well known feminine connotations in the misogynist sense (1983: 200/665). In contrast, life is presented in heroically masculine terms as a movement of ascent approaching freedom. It is not just Bergson's use of metaphor that is sexed; the very structure of the spatial relations Bergson that deploys in his image of duration as a monism has phallic connotations. Pure duration is at the summit of the Whole, while matter serves as the base.

III. Seminal Creativity

The sexed hierarchy in Bergson's formulation of the relationship between life and matter is perhaps most pronounced in his account of evolution. Paradoxically, the emergence of sexual generation, as such, receives scant attention in his description of evolution's dynamic progress.

Bergson posits the *élan vital* as a virtual multiplicity, which in its initial impulsion held an immense reservoir of forces within itself. These forces contained mutually antagonistic aspects. In order to allow them an ability to grow, the forces were obliged to split up into distinct tendencies. We have arrived at one of the central theses of Bergson's most famous work: evolution proceeds by means of dissociation (1983: 100/579–80). This process is nothing other than the acts by which the multiplicity of the *élan vital* is actualised. Evolution proceeds through the differentiating movement of duration, which draws on the *élan vital* to create distinct tendencies.

While Bergson does not ascribe a common purpose to life, the *élan vital* is understood monistically. It is the very force from which life arises (1983: 51/ 538). At this virtual source, all of the tendencies of life abided together because their features did not yet need to be differentiated. In Bergson's vision of the Whole as an incalculable multiplicity of different degrees of tension discussed earlier, the *élan vital* is virtually implied as the force of all of the different rhythms of duration.

Tendencies are not defined by the possession of particular attributes. On the contrary, they are characterised by the aspects that have the most emphasis. Animals, for instance, tend to accentuate movement while plants incline towards immobility. Most aspects of the Whole continue to abide in a specific tendency in a virtual state. 'There is no manifestation of life which does not contain in a rudimentary state – either latent or virtual – the essential characters of most other manifestations [translation modified]' (1983: 106/585). In this sense, something of the virtual Whole abides in all of the dissociated tendencies that make up life (1983: 54/540).

The first great bifurcation in Bergson's account of evolution is the division of the *élan vital* into life and matter. For Bergson, the reason for this dissociation is found in the divergent characters of these two tendencies. Life contains an unstable and explosive balance of forces to which inert matter is tremendously resistant (1983: 98/578). Their dissociation enabled these antagonistic aspects of the *élan vital* to express themselves. It is should be remembered: the *élan vital* is virtual. It functions as the 'reservoir' from which life engenders new tendencies, which in turn give rise to actualities. The emergence of matter and life, then, must be understood as an act of creation. When Bergson describes matter in negative terms, for instance, as the inversion or interruption of duration, he is speaking of it as a tendency distinguished from the inventive duration of life (1983: 186–271/653–725; Deleuze 1991: 100–3). Bergsonian matter is construed as a positive fact. Yet it is precisely the antagonism between the explosive force of life and the rhythm of near necessity found in the force of matter which led to their bifurcation. Matter was an obstacle to life's creative dynamism.

The dissociation between life and matter is the first of many bifurcations in the movement of evolution. Although Bergson doesn't say this explicitly, the first divergence within the tendency of life engenders what he calls 'sexual generation.' In a section of twelve pages devoted to the bifurcation between plant and animal, he makes a fleeting remark:

> sexual generation is perhaps only a luxury for the plant, but to the animal it was a necessity, and the plant must have been driven to it by the same *élan* which impelled the animal thereto, a primitive, original *élan* anterior to the separation of the two kingdoms [translation modified]. (1983: 119/596)

What I want to emphasise here is less the thesis that sexual reproduction is perhaps a luxury for plants, than Bergson's admission that this bifurcation arises from a 'primitive, original *élan*.' He readily admits that not all of the directions of life hold the same interest for him. Bergson is particularly concerned with the path that leads to 'Man' (*l'homme*) [sic] (1983: 105/584). Bergson's treatise on evolution thus attends carefully to the dissociation between plant and animal and the bifurcation between instinct and intellect. Yet his allusions to the emergence of sexual reproduction are few. Surely sexual generation occupies an important place in the path that leads to the human species?[7]

Bergson's marginalisation of sexual generation is interesting in relation to the sexed hierarchy I suggest is at work in the images and metaphors he draws upon to articulate his thought. In my view, emergence of the sexed hierarchy precedes the primitive *élan* that Bergson credits as the force that impels the emergence of sexual generation. I think it motivates the very desire to split the 'antagonistic' forces of life and matter. While Bergson largely abandons an analysis of sexual generation, he repeatedly invokes images of ejaculation, explosion and erection to account for the evolution the life and matter relation.

I alluded earlier to Bergson's use of a paternal metaphor to describe the genesis of the free act in *Time and Free Will*. In *The Creative Evolution* he draws upon the image of paternal creativity to elaborate another kind of free act, the organising act. While the free act characterises human consciousness, the organising act is fundamentally transhuman; its source is the *élan vital*. This act is particularly important because it creates complex structures such as the human eye. Bergson writes:

> The organizing act... has something explosive about it: it needs at the beginning the smallest possible place, a minimum of matter, as if the organizing forces only entered space reluctantly. The spermatozoon, which sets in motion the evolutionary process of the embryonic life, is one of the smallest cells of the organism; and it is only a small part of the spermatozoon that really takes part in the operation. (1983: 92/574)

This procreative image confers all of the creative force upon the purely temporal act which enters the space of matter 'only reluctantly.' In addition to emphasising the immateriality of the organising act here, Bergson's image downplays the materiality of sperm. It as though the truly creative aspect of sperm is not reducible to its material status.[8] This is, arguably, the most explicit use of a hierarchically sexed image in Bergson's account of evolution, yet there are many more instances in which he theorises the relationship between life and matter in sexist terms, at least implicitly.

In a particularly puzzling formulation, Bergson suggests that life is an immaterial force making itself, while matter is unmaking itself. Matter's tendency towards spatiality, or what Bergson calls extension, can be understood as a temporal tension that is interrupted. He proposes that matter should be imagined as a falling weight (1983: 245/703). Conversely life is a movement of ascent. These opposed movements must be understood together, especially given that, as Bergson admits, the creative activity of life evolves with matter on the surface of Earth. 'If it were pure consciousness, *a fortiori* if it were supraconsciousness, it would be pure creative activity' (1983: 245/703). This formulation suggests that life could exist independently of matter. Indeed, in the Huxley Lecture he makes precisely this claim (1922: 35/835).[9]

The evolution of life on Earth has always been attached to matter. Life is '*riveted* to an organism that *subjects* (*la soumet*) it to the general laws of inert matter. But everything happens as if it were doing its upmost to set itself free' (1983: 245/703). Bergson contends that life retards the descent of matter by acting upon matter with its explosive energy. He turns to the cholorophyllian function of plants. Plants accumulate energy, as in a reservoir, that can be discharged suddenly through the nervous systems of the animals that eat them. Bergson hypothesises that prior to the dissociation between plant and animal, life was accumulating 'explosives' to be released through movements. 'It is like an effort to raise the weight which falls' (1983: 246/704).

Matter is a weight that the explosive force of life attempts to mould and transform with tremendous effort. In my view, this scenario is reminiscent of a violent figuration of heterosexual intercourse in which a man fucks a woman whose inertia approaches 'absolute passivity' (1983: 200/665). Woman is figured here as an 'inert' weight acted upon by a frenzied man.

The phallocentrism of Bergson's life-matter relation is also evident in a number of images that he proposes for understanding the relation between them. He invokes his readers to think of a vessel full of steam at high pressure. The vessel has a few cracks and steam escapes its enclosure, in a jet:

> The steam shot (*lancée*) into the air is nearly all condensed into little drops which fall back (*retombent*), and this condensation and this fall (*chute*) represent simply the loss of something, an interruption, a deficit. But a small part of the jet stream subsists, uncondensed, for some seconds; it is making an effort to raise the drops which are falling (*tombent*); it succeeds at most in retarding (*ralentir*) their fall (*la chute*). So, from an immense reservoir of life, jets must be shooting out (*s'élancer*) unceasingly, of which each falling back (*retombent*) is a world [translation modified]. (1983: 247/705)

Bergson warns against taking this comparison too far. The cracks, the jets of steam, the forming of the drops are subject to the laws of inert matter and the creation of a world is a free act. So he proposes instead the image of the action of an arm raising itself. For Bergson, the effort to lift the arm gives a better sense of life's freedom, while the tendency of the arm to fall back down reveals the direction of matter unmaking this effort. 'In this image of a *creative action which unmakes itself* we ... have a more exact representation of [animate] matter' (1983: 247–8/705). This image, like that of jet stream shooting forth from a vessel, is reminiscent of a penis becoming erect in arousal and falling back into detumescence. And Bergson proposes yet another metaphor with strongly phallic connotations.

> Consciousness or supraconsciousness is the name for the rocket whose extinguished fragments (*les debris*) fall back as matter; consciousness ... is ... that which subsists of the rocket itself, passing through the fragments and lighting them up into organisms. (1983: 261/716)

'Inert' matter is the debris of the *élan vital's* immense effort to create. Some of this debris gets animated by the passage of consciousness through 'it' and thus engenders organisms. However, it is the tendency of life itself that is credited as the true creator of the living being.

In my view these passages demonstrate the valorisation of a hyper-masculine theory of life and corresponding devaluation of matter as feminine. This is not a binary hierarchy because Bergson's concepts of life and matter are never actualised as pure activity and pure space. He emphasises that there is always a trace of the characteristics of most other tendencies within any of the actualised tendencies of life (1983: 106/585). For this reason, matter's inclination towards pure repetition is never fully achieved. There are some oscillations in matter's rhythm that are analogous to the dynamic transformations articulated in the duration of life. At the same time, life is not manifested as pure creative energy. Life is riveted to matter, and can only actualise free acts through its inverse tendency. Moreover, Bergson admits that if materiality was pure repetition, consciousness could never have installed itself within matter's palpitations. In a key passage from the Huxley lecture, he writes:

> Life would be impossible were the determination of matter so absolute as to admit of no relaxation. Suppose, however, that at particular moments and at particular points matter shows a certain elasticity, then and there will be the opportunity for consciousness to install itself. It will have to humble itself at first; yet, once installed, it will dilate, it will spread from its point of entry and not rest till it has conquered (*obtenir*) the whole, for time is at its disposal, and the slightest quantity of indetermination, by continually adding to itself, will make up as much freedom as you like. (1920: 18/824–5)

At particular moments, matter 'offers a certain elasticity' that allows life to transform it. Consciousness could never have succeeded in creating organisms without the emergence of these fluctuations at certain points within matter's rhythm. A number of important questions emerge from this passage that Bergson does not address. Why does matter generate fluctuations in its rhythm? Is elasticity merely a fortuitous accident or are the oscillations in matter provoked when consciousness seeks to install an action upon it? Does this imply that matter anticipates the imminence of a new act, which exceeds the plane of actuality that Bergson frequently insists matter is confined to? We could say what Bergson does not say: when the force of consciousness stimulates matter, it does not merely repeat its past. Matter actualises alterations in its tension that constitute new configurations in the becoming of the world. But this is still to accept the terms of Bergson's dualism. Perhaps we would do better to reconsider the life-matter relation beyond dualism?

Let us return to what Bergson says in this quotation. Far from modifying the violent hierarchy of life over matter by allowing matter, however infinitesimally, to participate in engendering new actualities in the world, Bergson declares that material elasticity allows consciousness to install itself. Once consciousness has entered matter, 'it will not rest until it has conquered the whole' (1920: 18/824). In sexed terms, matter's elasticity makes her amenable to the power of the masculine tendency to create. She offers herself to life and allows him 'to conquer' (*obtenir*) her.

Given the sexual violence of Bergson's figuration of the life-matter relation, it is no surprise to find him asserting that the subjugation of matter is most successful in 'Man' (*l'homme*). In the same essay, Bergson praises 'man alone' for his ability to force matter into the status of a 'mere instrument' (*à l'état d'instrument*). He has this ability because he can oppose every habit he has contracted with a contrary habit and this gives him more freedom to act upon matter than any other animate creature.[10] In other organisms, freedom remains riveted to the 'chains' of matter. At most they are able to stretch these chains.' But, in Man, 'a sudden bound (*un saut brusque*) is made.' Freedom is unleashed. 'Freedom, coming to itself whilst necessity is at grips with itself, brings back matter to the condition of being a mere instrument. It is as though it has divided in order to rule' (1920: 26/830).

For Bergson, Man is distinguished from animals by a difference in nature and presented as the 'end' of evolution. He warns his readers that Man is the 'end' in a special sense. Bergson does not mean to imply that Man's success realises a ready-made plan. The divergent actualisations of the *élan vital* were contingent and radically unpredictable. Man is only one species among a number of them. Nonetheless, Man is the great success of evolution because he alone allowed life to finally triumph over the 'obstacle' of matter (1983: 263–6/718–21). Despite his argument to the contrary, Bergson's celebration of Man as the 'end' of evolution" tends to undercut the innovation for which his philosophy is justly famous: the claim that duration articulates an incalculable flow of novelty (1983: 266/720–1).

Keith Ansell-Pearson has voiced grave reservations about these humanist assertions in Bergson's corpus. According to Ansell-Pearson Bergson's evolutionary philosophy elevates the 'form' of Man in a gesture of 'residual perfectionism' (Ansell-Pearson 1999: 158–9). I support Ansell-Pearson's call to move beyond the 'residual perfectionism' and 'anthropocentrism' at work in this aspect of Bergson's *oeuvre* (Ansell-Pearson 1999: 159). But it is not just a case of exceeding the problematic elevation of 'Man' in Bergsonism. The privilege conferred upon life as a movement of ascent and creation and the simultaneous degradation of matter as an obstacle to the progress of life must be called into question. This violent hierarchy articulates a kind of phallic anthropomorphism, where matter is the stuff or dead weight that paternal life must impregnate or overcome in order to incarnate animate beings and introduce free acts into the world. At his most extreme, Bergson valorises a spiritual position that is nothing short of somataphobic. He speculates that human consciousness may have 'an intenser life' no longer riveted to the body (Bergson 1920: 35/ 835).

IV. Rethinking Material Elasticity

I have suggested that Bergson's split between life and matter is bound up in the disavowal of a hierarchical conception of sexual difference. The implications of this split are troubling, not only from a feminist perspective, but also a philosophical approach that seeks to affirm the dynamism and duration of matter.

Manuel de Landa's thought strikes me as a promising resource in rethinking Bergsonian materiality. He draws upon complexity theory that has shown matter's capacity to exceed the tendency towards entropy in far from equilibrium conditions. In these instances, 'inert' matter is capable of organising itself and acting in ways that exceed mathematical prediction. For de Landa this suggests that 'matter can "express" itself in complex and creative ways' (de Landa 1992: 133). He emphasises that the virtual arises from the duration of matter. This is not to say that the virtual is actualised; it means that the virtual has a material foundation, or better, it arises from a material rhythm.[11]

I do not think this is strictly unfaithful to Bergson. In *Matter and Memory*, Bergson describes the Whole as 'concrete extensity' pervaded by, '*modifications, perturbations* changes of *tension* or of *energy* and nothing else' (1981: 201). In this monistic formulation life and matter might be thought together as enduring tensions capable of actualising the new.

References

Ansell-Pearson, Keith (1999) 'Bergson and Creative Evolution/Involution: Exposing the Transcendental Illusion of Organismic Life', in John Mullarkey (ed.), *The New Bergson*, Manchester: Manchester University Press, pp. 146–67.

Bergson, Henri (1913) *Time and Free Will: An Essay on the Immediate Data of Consciousness*, trans. F. L. Pogson, London: George Allen.

Bergson, Henri (1920) *Mind-Energy*, trans. H. Wildon Carr, New York: Henry Holt.

Bergson, Henri (1959) *Oeuvres*, Paris: PUF.

Bergson, Henri (1981) *Matter and Memory*, trans. Nancy Margaret Paul and W. Scott Palmer, New York: Zone.

Bergson, Henri (1983) *The Creative Evolution*, trans. Arthur Mitchell, Lanham, MD: UPA.

Bergson, Henri (1992) *The Creative Mind An Introduction to Metaphysics*, trans. Mabelle L. Andison. New York: Citadel.

De Landa, Manuel (1992) 'Nonorganic Life', in Jonathan Crary and Sanford Kwinter (eds), *Incorporations: Zone 6*, New York: Zone, pp. 129–67.

De Landa, Manuel (2002) *Intensive Science and Virtual Philosophy*, New York: Continuum.

Deleuze, Gilles (1990) *Bergsonism*, trans. Hugh Tomlinson and Barbara Habberjam, New York: Zone Books.

Hill, Rebecca (2008) 'Interval, sexual difference: Irigaray and Bergson', *Hypatia*, 23:1, pp. 119–31.

May, William (1970) 'The Reality of Matter in the Metaphysics of Bergson', *International Philosophical Quarterly*, X, pp. 611–42.

Watson, Irene (2002) 'Aboriginal Laws and the Sovereignty of *Terra Nullius*', *Borderlands*, 1:2, http://www.borderlandsejournal.adelaide.edu.au/vol1no2_2002/watson_laws.html.

Notes

1. All references are to the English translations of Bergson's work. The second page reference refers to French edition of Bergson's *Oeuvres* (1959).
2. For a close reading of this remark in Bergson see my 'Interval, sexual difference: Irigaray and Bergson' (2008).
3. Reflection upon the 'inner life of the self' is the cornerstone of Bergson's intuitive deduction of duration. This procedure is first elaborated in *Time and Free Will*. Bergson presents this as purely temporal. Contra Bergson, I ague that that the deduction of duration is a both embodied and sexuate in 'Interval, sexual difference: Irigaray and Bergson' (2008).
4. William E. May argues that the limit of pure freedom described in this passage is how Bergson conceives of God (1970: 637).
5. As I have already indicated, it is only in his first book, *Time and Free Will*, that Bergson identifies matter with pure space. In all of his subsequent publications, the absolute passivity sketched in this passage is a pure limit beyond the actual. See May 1970: 614–5.
6. It is noteworthy that, in this instance, Bergson defines materiality, without qualification, as *pure* repetition. In the passages from *The Creative Evolution* I have just discussed, Bergson says matter stops short of *pure* repetition. The passage comes from his important essay 'An Introduction to Metaphysics' (Bergson 1992: 159–200) which was published several years after *Matter and Memory*, but before *The Creative Evolution*.
7. Bergson refers to 'sexuality' in the first chapter of *The Creative Evolution*. He also makes a few references to sex cells (59–60/ 563–4; 79–80/545–6). The neglect of this primitive differentiation is even more marked in Deleuze's reading of *The Creative Evolution*. Deleuze provides a diagram summarising the divergence of the *élan vital* into distinct actualities but omits what Bergson calls 'sexual generation' (Deleuze 1988: 102).
8. It is perhaps unfair to chastise Bergson for neglecting to mention the egg in this image. After all, the active part played by ovum in the selection of sperm to create an embryo was not discovered until the second half of the twentieth century.
9. Bergson speculates that the mind may outlive the body. He suggests that living in the conventional sense may prepare consciousness for 'more efficient action, an intenser life', no longer harnessed to the matter of the body (1920: 35/835).
10. Bergson also identifies the complexity of the human brain, social life and languages in his argument for Man's superiority over of life forms on this planet (1983: 264–5/719–20).
11. De Landa's excellent discussion of the scientific background to Deleuze's conception of multiplicity is a particularly valuable contribution to this field. See especially chapter one 'The Mathematics of the Virtual: Manifolds, Vector Field and Transformation Groups' (De Landa 2002: 9–55).

DOI: 10.3366/E1750224108000391

Reviews

Rosi Braidotti (2002) *Metamorphoses: Towards a Feminist Theory of Becoming*, Cambridge: Polity Press.

Rosi Braidotti (2006) *Transpositions: On Nomadic Ethics*, Cambridge: Polity Press.

A desire for an affirmative and invigorating concept of identity, relations and ethics within feminism in these 'strange times'[1] where 'strange things are happening'[2] forms the generative *modus operandum* in Rosi Braidotti's complementary sister-contributions to critical theory. Indeed, the acknowledged strangeness of contemporary Western spatio-temporal subjects forms one of the crucial tenets in Braidotti's emancipatory agenda. *Metamorphoses* and *Transpositions* develop a strategy formed on Irigaray's emphasis on the importance of sexual difference and constructive materialism, and achieved through a Deleuzian conception of simultaneity and nomadism. Subjectivity is, for Braidotti, always already in motion and bodies and spaces are materialised in the act of becoming different or strange. The significant task of a nomadic feminist ethics is to harness and relish bodies' capacities for transformation and to discover their potential for mapping flux, in shaping localised traces of becoming.

Braidotti thus prepares a conceptual space where the de-essentialised subject of Western deconstructivist thinking can take pleasure from and explore the possibilities of social construction and material being. She provides a possibility of 'multiple singularities without fixed identities'[3] in the act of 'legitimating and representing a multi-centred, internally differentiated female feminist subjectivity without falling into relativism or fragmentation'[4]. These singularities are, however, not singular stand-alone concepts, nor is the subjective space plane. 'Just like travellers can capture the "essential lines" of landscape or of a place in the speed of crossing it, this is not superficiality, but a way of framing the longitudinal and latitudinal forces that structure a certain spatio-temporal "moment".'[5]

In emphasising corporeal experience and refuting both a coherently essential and a purely superficial idea of the sexed and/or gendered body, Braidotti forms a concept that is not in opposition to, but goes beyond both the third and the second waves of feminism. Is Braidotti's project signalling the emergence of a fourth wave of feminism; or even a form of feminism which should be conceived of outside of the linearity of conceptive 'waves'?

Although Braidotti shares a conception of gender constructivity with certain third wave feminist philosophies, she differentiates her viewpoint from less materialist feminist thought, such as is formulated in the early work of Judith Butler. Braidotti argues that there are certain socially constructed identity-shaping loci of becoming, but these are cartographical points within inter-, trans- or internal materialising processes rather than external impositions. She allows that 'To enact different steps of this process of becoming, one has to work on the conceptual coordinates,'[6] but these never remain superficial. The types of transformations that Butler urges onto the body remain figural, because processes of becoming 'are neither easily accessible nor free of pain. In other words, changes hurt and transformations are painful; this does not mean that they are deprived of positive and even pleasurable side-effects, of course.'[7]

The affective facet of transformative bodily positioning – or what may more appropriately be termed transpositioning – is a vital element in Braidotti's project. Metamorphoses and Transpositions encounter a number of cultural amalgamative becomings, such as becoming-woman/animal/insect/machine/cyborg/other, considering these as 'process[es] of intersecting forces (affects) and spatio-temporal variables (connections)'.[8] Through the produced affects each process of becoming is connected to other processes of becoming at loci of empathetically joint and shared sensation. 'A "location", in fact, is not a self-appointed and self-designed subject-position. It is a collectively shared and constructed, jointly occupied spatio-temporal territory.'[9] She establishes that 'These multi-layered levels of affectivity are the building blocks for creative transpositions, which compose a plane of actualization of relations, that is to say points of contact between self and surroundings.'[10]

Rhizomatic affect is thus the means by which the subjective becomes general and the general becomes subjective. It comprises the cartographical points of becoming-world and becoming-ethical. Braidotti refers to works from the schools of eco-feminism and viral politics, developing a theory of shared affect or 'care', where 'anti-essentialist yet vitalistic figurations'[11] prepare space for 'a model of porosity, fluidity, multiple interconnections and symbolic interrelation, a transversal subjectivity'.[12] These figurations are 'hybrid figurations',[13] a stand-alone complex, requiring transpositioning processes of becoming, which 'negotiate with the generative powers of *zoe*, this life in "me" which does not bear my name and does not even fully qualify as human'.[14] Braidotti returns to Deleuze and Guattari and the concept of the Body-without-Organs or incorporeal, arguing that the process of becoming-ethical starts where a 'primacy is given to the Relation over the terms'[15]: it is the becoming of 'the affective being of the middle, the interconnection, the Relation'.[16]

Braidotti's notion of ethics is a process that has nothing to do with either dominant morality or relativism: 'Rather it contains clearly set limits that are activated by careful negotiations.'[17] She argues that 'To accept differential boundaries does not condemn us to relativism, but to the necessity to negotiate each passage.'[18] Becoming-ethical involves an affirmation of the limits and boundaries-in-shaping. They need to be considered 'points of encounter and not of closure: living boundaries and not fixed walls'.[19]

For feminism, as well as for any other emancipatory discourse, Rosi Braidotti's project opens up an alternative to the 'loss, failure, melancholia and ontological lack',[20] which she claims to be central to much contemporary, especially psycho-analytic, theoretical discussion. It presents an opportunity to pursue a political agenda without adhering to fusty binary power structures. One may question what happens after the living boundaries have been embraced: once we are celebratory participants of the process of becoming-affirmative, what happens next? However, I believe that this question belongs to a future configuration within the theorising negotiation that Rosi Braidotti is taking part in.

Karin Sellberg
University of Edinburgh
DOI: 10.3366/E1750224108000408

Notes

1. Braidotti, *Metamorphoses*, p. 1.
2. Ibid. p. 1.
3. Ibid. p. 149.
4. Ibid. p. 26.
5. Braidotti, *Transpositions*, p. 172.
6. Ibid. p. 169.

7. Braidotti, *Metamorphoses*, p. 43.
8. Ibid. p. 21.
9. Ibid. p. 12.
10. Braidotti, *Transpositions*, p. 172.
11. Ibid. p. 123.
12. Ibid. p. 123.
13. Ibid. p. 123.
14. Ibid. p. 123.
15. Ibid. p. 129.
16. Ibid. p. 129.
17. Ibid. p. 268.
18. Ibid. p. 268.
19. Ibid. p. 268.
20. Braidotti, *Metamorphoses*, p. 57.

Martin-Jones, David (2006) *Deleuze, Cinema and National Identity: Narrative Time in National Contexts*, Edinburgh: Edinburgh University Press, 256 pages.

David Martin-Jones's cinematic application of Deleuze as a form of 'philosophical sodomy' is provocative from the outset. His distinctive assemblage of the time–image, the movement-image and the politics of national identity is bound to fuel ongoing arguments that reverberate beyond the field of theory. As Martin-Jones indicates, film scholars remain 'bemused' by or 'concerned' about Deleuze's value to their field. This is particularly the case with Anglo-American film studies. The book intervenes in the long–standing and often highly partisan debate between formalism (film as art form and aesthetic experience) and culturalism (film as representational socio-political practice). In tandem with this, opposing camps often contest the relative political values of 'experimental', frequently modernist-inflected art and popular genres.

Deleuze's position as a Parisian cinéaste with a predilection for the art-house canon is well known and has been contested, both by lovers of both popular mainstream film and world cinema. As Martin-Jones and others have reminded us, Deleuze's personal view of film history is predominantly Eurocentric. The majority of his examples are modernist–inflected works from European art film and 'deviant' Hollywood directors such as Welles, and he locates the birth of the time-image in the new waves that developed in the wake of post-war Italian neo-realism. Deleuze's approach to Japanese directors such as Ozu and Mizoguchi is philosophical/aesthetic rather than being motivated by the politics of Japanese nationalism.

Yet of course Deleuze and Guattari's joint work is overtly informed by an astutely radical political awareness espousing micropolitical oppositions to local, international and global abuses of power. Actively involved in the events May 1968 and their aftermath, Deleuze and Guattari do not indulge in pure aestheticism, though they certainly privilege art as a potentially radicalising force. Seeking to refute both psychic interiority and fixed semantic systems, Deleuze and Guattari insist that art is an immanent process 'a being in sensation and nothing else: it exists in itself' (1994: 164). Art 'undoes the triple organisation of perceptions, affections, and opinions in order to substitute a monument composed of percepts, affects, and blocs of sensation' that replace language (1994: 176). By this apparent refutation of ideological content, Deleuze and Guattari advocate looking elsewhere than representational equations or Oedipal symbolism. Schizoanalytic approaches to art thus replace representation by material capture. Deleuze's cinematic applications seek an experiential rather than a significatory approach to the moving image; one that deterritorialises perception via the machinic automatism of the medium.

As Martin–Jones indicates, the 'localised historical dimension' is deliberately absent from Deleuze's solo work on cinema. Using this absence as a motivation for his own exploration of film and national identity, he expands the parameters of the cinema books by drawing on relevant insights from the works co–authored with Guattari. For Deleuze and Guattari, the forces of reterritorialisation and deterritorialisation are much more than an intense aesthetic encounter. Rather than being for its own sake, art is always intended as 'a tool for blazing life lines'. Here, the strengths of Martin–Jones's critique emerge, as he uses his film readings to express a politically-committed analysis of shifting international power-relations. Setting out to link formalism and culturalism with philosophy, he puts the forces of Deleuzian theory to work in an engaged and engaging critique of national identities in recent films.

Martin-Jones begins with Deleuze's location of the time-image in the cinema of post-1945 Europe, with its fragmentation of linear narrative time. His response to these more labyrinthine forms of narrative is also marked by David Bordwell's very different typology of film based on the classification of narrative structures. Despite its structuralist and cognitive approach, Bordwell's category of the parametric art–film has, arguably, some commonality of content, though not of perspective, with Deleuze's own cinematic taxonomy. The book's case-studies are chiefly generic hybrids such as *Eternal Sunshine of the Spotless Mind* (Michael Gondry, 2004) that mix independent/art house devices with popular box-office appeal. Other Deleuzian film theorists (among them, Patricia

Pisters, Barbara Kennedy and myself) also find this type of hybrid film very productive for Deleuzian-inflected explorations, but Martin-Jones is consistently led by the distinct socio-political focus on national identity.

Deleuze, who elsewhere discusses 'minor literature', introduces the concept of 'minor cinema' in *Cinema 2: The Time-Image* (1989). As Martin-Jones notes, Deleuze's consideration of films by John Cassavetes, Jean Rouch and Charles Perrault does not overtly address issues of national identity per se. Rather than pursuing this agenda, Deleuze discovers in these films a different 'revolutionary' challenge to move beyond subjective identity. The rhizomatic processes of becomings–other move instead towards a more radical embrace of collective identity, which may or may not be nationally motivated.

The time-image exceeds fragmented narrative form and politically explicit thematic content. Asserting that 'the brain is the screen' (in his eponymous essay), Deleuze argues that by bringing 'a little time in its pure state' onto the screen and breaking up conventional narrative patterns, it offers a temporal hiatus with potential to trigger new thought and new forms of micropolitical engagement. This distinct political focus could explain Deleuze's 'reticence' about dealing with macropolitical issues of nationhood per se in the context of the cinema books. Yet, rather than following this line of enquiry, Martin-Jones re-works major national discourses and 'minor actions' to produce an original ideological analysis of narrative strategies in selected films. He develops his tightly constructed agenda by locating major/minor forces in the same films and revealing their antithetical dynamics at work in a struggle for national identity. *Deleuze, Cinema and National Identity* offers a clear and accessible introduction to Deleuze's two main categories of cinematic time. It provides ample textual examples to anchor chief concepts and to key in the subsequent argument. The structure of the exposition is rigorously constructed and its direction is frequently signposted. It develops dialectically along the clear trajectory of a series of contested binaries: movement-image/time-image, major/minor, and reterritorialisation/deterritorialisation.

One area in which Martin-Jones takes creative liberties with Deleuze appears in his alignment of the movement-image to an unproblematic presentation of national narrative time, and the time-image to 'multiple, jumbled or reversed' narrative time that expresses national struggles. He strikingly asserts that the contested ground of movement and time make these films either 'time images caught in the act of becoming movement-images' or 'movement-images caught in the act of becoming time-images'. Yet rather than staging such a battle of clearly opposed forces, Deleuze's account reveals a complex intermeshed taxonomy that puts certain films and directors to work across both books. Deleuzian film theory, in its focus on the ontological properties of the medium, is applicable in some degree to *all* films, regardless of explicit subject-matter, style or genre. Movement and time in cinema inevitably use both temporality and movement as their modus operandi. Film images move in time and the interlinked process of the brain's own temporally moving images problematises dialectically neat divisions at both macro and micro levels.

In a productive move, Martin-Jones links Deleuze's two-plane model of temporality and Homi Bhabha's conceptualisation of national identity formation via 'rhetorical figures' that produce a double time-structure: the technological and progressive present and the timeless past. One contentious issue here is that Bhabha's rhetorical figures are emblematic but Deleuze's cinematic figures are stylistic devices that operate elsewhere than overt image content. Nevertheless, as Martin-Jones indicates, Bhabha selects the stylistically experimental *Handsworth Songs* (John Akomfra 1986) to argue that the film's presentation of successive waves of immigrants to the UK disrupts the homogenising tendency of national discourse. Overall, though, the political specificity of Bhabha's ideological concepts does not align neatly with either Bordwell's Classic Realist Text/parametric narration or Deleuze's movement and time images. Again, Martin-Jones's argument challenges us to dialectical activity by making new theoretical assemblages.

The first chapter provides a clear, workable outline of Deleuze's cinematic applications of Bergsonian memory. This is connected with the national theme via the occluded contexts of racial Mexican anxiety (Hitchcock's *Vertigo*, 1958) and the displaced status of Catholic heritage in the Italy of 'the economic miracle' in Fellini's 1963 film $8\frac{1}{2}$. Here, Martin-Jones unfolds a confidently handled series of parallels between film text and ideological context more typically associated with sociohistorical and culturalist approaches to film studies. He thus sets up and seeks to integrate two distinct frames of reference in a way that neither 'party' might find entirely satisfactory but which throws us the gauntlet to engage with further reflection on the limitations of these respective agendas when working with film.

Martin-Jones further explores national identity via contemporaneous fantasies of the global city as progressive, egalitarian marketplace, as seen in Nora Ephron's 1998 *You've got Mail*. His focal cities are

London in Peter Howitt's *Sliding Doors* (1997) and Berlin in Tom Tykwer's German film, *Run, Lola Run* (2000). Here he interrogates the relations of time and memory, connecting labyrinthine narrative structures relevant to changing national contexts. In his reading of *Sliding Doors*, Martin–Jones considers the Americanisation of London and its implications in relation to national memory loss. In *Run Lola Run*, the focus is on the reconstructed post-wall Berlin. He asserts that its centrality as meeting place of global networks and its embrace of materialist values is conveyed via the film's 'fractal' structure. Both films remove evidence of their location city's representative national past and replace this with vibrant contemporaneous images of internationalism unmarked by problematic issues of ethnicity. At the same time, films like *Sliding Doors* use nostalgic notions of quintessential Englishness as a 'structuring absence', evinced by the casting of American star Gwyneth Paltrow and her adopted 'plummy home Counties accent'.

The argument shifts focus to a different national scenario, tackling two cinematic takes on the first Gulf War and American triumphalism: *Memento* (Christopher Nolan, 2000) and *Saving Private Ryan* (Steven Spielberg, 1998). *Saving Private Ryan* remains closer to a conventional narrative with flashbacks. Deleuze analyses the temporal complexities of flashback in the films of Joseph Mankiewicz and others. Martin-Jones here aligns them with the time-image as the implications of American national memory are re–fashioned and mythologised via narrative discontinuities. Through an ethnically diverse group of soldiers, the film presents American diasporas as united in the 'quest to save America', drawing 'historical' inspiration from the Civil War and Abraham Lincoln's address.

Martin-Jones indicates that the film makes Deleuze's any-space-whatevers literally visible via location images of devastated European cities. He deploys the movement–image to equate the linear order of the troops with American political order as it seeks to control and realign the chaotic breakdown of social structures wrought by war. For Deleuze, though, the complex and shifting formation that is the movement-image is far from being unproblematically repressive. His main concern is to highlight and explore the category's diverse capacities to stimulate particular types of perception and concept formation via the multi-layered reverberations of affective forces in the screen/brain assemblage.

The nationally inflected reading of *Memento* has less overtly Deleuzian currency. This temporally and subjectively labyrinthine film is placed in Martin-Jones's category of movement-image 'caught in the act' of becoming time-image. Here, his interpretation is rendered more speculative than the previous case-study. He aligns the protagonist's personal 'getting away with murder' and the Gulf War via an allegorical use of the oil refinery setting. This kind of parable-construction engages worthwhile speculation but is less obviously Deleuzian in its inspiration.

The mainstream movement-image film *Terminator 3* (Jonathan Mostow, 2003) figures in Martin-Jones's analysis of the apocalyptic mood triggered by 9/11. He addresses more complex narratives via the 'structuring absence', a tactic that evokes psychoanalytical scenarios of the play of absence and presence. The Deleuze/Bergsonian 'Elsewhere', however, is outside or between the frame's represented content. It is durational not macropolitically representational in its ideological intent. The author makes the case that the 'structuring absence' of triumphalist narratives is 'smuggled in' to films that appear to be about time and personal memory. From Martin–Jones's perspective, these exemplify the time–image becoming movement–image. In the light of this thesis, in *Eternal Sunshine of the Spotless Mind*, post 9/11 paranoia seeks to reterritorialise the film's labyrinthine time–image with a homogenised model of national identity. Confusing narrative patterns retaliate by deterritorialisation as they struggle to keep national identity fragmented. The theme of memory erasure is Martin-Jones's other focal point. He maps the need to return to the causes of 9/11 onto Joel's and Clementine's quest to piece the past together after amnesia via the device of an audio-tape. Again, this reading deploys national allegory in intriguing, but perhaps not-strictly-Deleuzian ways.

An important element of the book's agenda is to extend Deleuzian applications not just to previously untheorised recent Western films, but to international cinemas outside the strictly Deleuzian canon. The less familiar we are with a culture and its national identities the more likely we are to rely on media images of that culture, including fictional feature films. Chapter Five analyses films from the Pacific Rim. Here, Martin–Jones offers a strongly argued reading of the play of possibilities and narrative oscillations between deterritorialisation and reterritorialisation. His political and ideological contextualisation is informed by sharp-eyed identification of the salient features in each country's twentieth and twenty first century political past.

The Cantonese gangster comedy *Too Many ways to be Number One* (Ka-fai Wai, 1997) convincingly indicates how the twice repeated narrative can be used to reconsider the handover of Hong Kong to China. Martin-Jones return to firmer ground here as he acknowledges the film's overt use of allegory regarding the choices of Hong Kong's population to throw in their lot with China or with Taiwan, both with attendant fears of national erasure. For Martin–Jones this is a 'time-image caught in the act of becoming a movement-image'. As before, his assertion is based on the equation of the time–image with non-linear narrative structure and an open ending. Here, the protagonist's emblematic choices of death (reincorporation with mainland China) or disability (throwing in its lot with Taiwan) is a decision deliberately left unresolved at the end of the film.

The Japanese film *Chaos* (Hideo Nakata, 1999) presents its narrative outcomes before their causes. Martin-Jones uses the jumbled and ambiguous narrative structure to problematise gender issues. He signals that the film's recollection-images have similarities to those of *Vertigo* in terms of the plot's 'indiscernible female double'. The narrative confusion between Satomi as femme fatale and Saori as dutiful wife is viewed as representative of the changing roles of women in contemporary Japan. Satomi's leap from the cliff, temporally frozen on freeze frame, is thus presented as a microcosm of the ambiguity of women's roles and possibilities in the nation's future.

New Korean cinema is illustrated by Chang-dong Lee's 2000 *Peppermint Candy*, a fictionalised scrutiny of South Korea's national narrative over two decades, hence its deployment of a less open-ended narrative structure than the previous films in this section. *Peppermint Candy*'s allegorical intent is made overt, but is rendered more complex by a reverse narrative. Martin-Jones suggests that moments of potential change are signalled by the character's temporary sensory-motor incapacity as manifest in a limp. The protagonist Yong-ho's potentially Bergsonian search in the past to find an image that matches the present is indicated, but Martin-Jones's deployment of the time-image remains consistently macropolitical rather than philosophical in its remit.

The underlying theoretical trajectories of Martin-Jones's thesis retain clear acknowledged links with Bordwell's narrative schema and Comolli and Narboni's categories of politically motivated film form. His readings privilege the films' representational narrative content above the expressive style of images, their affects, percepts and the new mental concepts to which these give rise. Yet, as part of the temporal hiatus between perception and action, the affective interval is crucial to thinking Deleuzian aesthetics and its impact on us. Affect is strongly and horribly operant in some of Martin-Jones's examples: the torture sequences in *Peppermint Candy* immediately spring to mind, and a further consideration might have encountered significant layers of perceptual and conceptual response as well as the important focus on represented content.

His argument that some films reterritorialise the time-image by defining national identity through the movement–image and deterritorialise the movement-image by the reverse process sets up a sharply dialectical contest between these categories that initially appears very different from Deleuze's multivalent taxonomic agenda. Yet, this deliberately chosen critical distance offers us in itself a productive hiatus for further thought. Deleuze and Guattari's perspectives encourage innovative development rather than purely scholarly exegesis. The cinema books are concerned with how rather than what we think and how this might be changed. Rather than producing another philosophical explication of Deleuze's Eurocentrically inflected cinema books, *Deleuze, Cinema and National Identity* mobilises their concepts by engaging them in critical and creative action in a crucial new field.

Overall, Martin-Jones's book raises some crucial questions on the nature of Deleuzian-inflected critique and its use/value for film studies. He argues indubitably that we need to increase the scope of Deleuze's theories to include the shifting fabric of cinematic work produced by nations in process. A consideration of this diverse and widely viewed range of films is timely. With their complex forces of deterritorialisation and reterritorialisation, generic conventions and formal experiments, they map out '*undecidable alternatives* between circles of past, *inextricable differences* between peaks of present' as time-image components gravitate against the extrinsic sensory-motor links of movement-images.

Martin-Jones reiterates his priorities of his thesis in the book's conclusion: to use Deleuze's film-theory to 'add another dimension to our understanding of the way national identity is constructed in cinema'. His ideologically engaged and systematically structured discussion links areas of inquiry often at loggerheads, philosophy, aesthetics, politics and history, to find ways they might co-operate as a viable assemblage. By moving from the letter to the spirit of Deleuzian critique, Martin-Jones's lucid, impressively argued book makes a provocative intervention in both Deleuze studies and film studies. This distinctive and politically engaged assemblage demands our closest attention.

Anna Powell
Manchester Metropolitan University
DOI: 10.3366/E175022410800041X

References

Deleuze, Gilles (1989) *Cinema 2: The Time-Image*, trans. Hugh Tomlinson and Barbara Habberjam, London: Athlone.
Deleuze, Gilles and Félix, Guattari (1994) *What is Philosophy?*, trans. Hugh Tomlinson and Graham Burchell, London, Verso.

Christian Kerslake (2007), *Deleuze and the Unconscious*, London and New York: Continuum, 246 pages.

This work arrives as the first book-length study devoted to examining Deleuze's relationship to various conceptions of the unconscious, psychoanalytic or otherwise. Anyone interested in this question would be well advised to consult the wealth of bibliographical and historical information that Kerslake has gathered together and, like him, not to neglect Deleuze's more 'esoteric' references which, as *Deleuze and the Unconscious* so forcefully shows, are undeniably present in his work. The originality of Kerslake's project is striking. It does, however, also present several shortcomings.

The first, perhaps minor, shortcoming relates to the ultimate aims of the book. Indeed, the title of the book is a little misleading since, as Kerslake admits, the 'book is not a general introduction to Deleuze (or even to Deleuze and the unconscious)' (3). The most appropriate description of the purpose of the book is, then, Kerslake's own, less encompassing one: 'a series of attempted raids on Deleuze's hive of ideas about the unconscious' (3). But what guides these 'raids', since there are, as Kerslake admits, 'plenty of omissions and probably lots of oversights too' (3)? Kerslake tells us from the outset that he will not deal with *Anti-Oedipus* (1983), since a very good introduction to this text has already been published (see Eugene Holland 1999), and since he is trying to uncover the theoretical background to that work. This is, of course, all well and good. But then we must wonder why he omits without explanation an examination of Deleuze's early references to Lacan in *Difference and Repetition* (1994), *The Logic of Sense* (1990a) and 'How Do We Recognize Structuralism?' (1998), for example; or why he does not examine Deleuze's sustained engagement with psychoanalysis in the second half of *The Logic of Sense*, which includes long analyses of the works of Freud, Klein, Leclaire, Laplanche and Pontalis, and so on. Based on the material examined by Kerslake, it seems that the Deleuzian ideas about the unconscious in which he is most interested relate to Deleuze's most obscure, esoteric, and even 'disavowed' references: Bergson's theory of instinct, Carl Jung, Johann Malfatti, and so on. However, given that these references are comparatively marginal to the Deleuzian corpus, scholars interested not only in the question of 'Deleuze and the unconscious', but also in Deleuze's pre-*Anti-Oedipus* takes on psychoanalysis and the unconscious, would perhaps be entitled to question the merit of devoting an entire book to their examination.

In any case, in what amounts to a highly original undertaking in its own right, Kerslake primarily wants to show that Deleuze's work is based in part on certain esoteric ideas about the unconscious (184). Indeed, he often expresses himself on this point in very strong terms.[1] However, examining the text, we can be dissatisfied with the strength of these claims for several reasons.

First of all, on several occasions, Kerslake moves without ample justification from the postulation of highly speculative 'genealogical' hypotheses to the unreserved affirmation of these hypotheses. For example, Kerslake deciphers in one of Jung's lectures on 'archetypes', a lecture that Deleuze appears to have read, the 'mention of "*a priori* conditions for fantasy-production"... as gesturing to a possible connection with Kant's theory of productive imagination'. He then proceeds to assert that, since archetypes take the form of problems, and since 'Deleuze's aim [in *Difference and Repetition* and in his work on Kant] is to show how the productive imagination is ultimately a receptacle for the harnessing of problematic Ideas., it 'can be *argued* that Deleuze takes up [Jung's] model in his theory of problematic Ideas in *Difference and Repetition*' (91–92 – my emphasis). To highlight this as a *possibility* is well and good. But it is quite another thing when, a few pages later, noting Deleuze's *only* substantial reference to Jung in *Difference and Repetition* – a footnote of uncertain value, to which we will return below – Kerslake fully affirms that Deleuze does indeed take up Jung's model, even going so far as to assert the Jungian '*origins*' of certain aspects of Deleuze's theory of the unconscious (96; 100). Indeed, in the absence of any analysis of the concept of the 'problem' such as it appears in *Difference and Repetition* – and to which, without mentioning Jung at all, most of the fourth chapter is devoted – this seems to be at best a rather exaggerated claim. What is more, in *Difference and Repetition*, when Deleuze does talk concretely about unconscious problems in the context of psychoanalysis, he predominately talks in Lacanian-structuralist terms about the displacement of the virtual object or 'phallus' in differential series, in the manner of Lacan's analysis of *The Purloined Letter* (Deleuze 1994: 106–7). We can thus be dissatisfied not only that Kerslake moves with only limited justification from very interesting genealogical speculations to their unequivocal affirmation, but also that he does not discuss certain other, and perhaps more pertinent, 'conceptual components' of the Deleuzian differential unconscious.

Besides Jungianism, Kerslake tracks down and argues for the persistence of several other 'esoteric' references in Deleuze's work. For instance, based on the selection of texts that Deleuze made for the collection *Instincts et Institutions* (1953), and on the short article 'De Sacher-Masoch au masochisme' (1961) where Deleuze turns in part to the Jungian coupling of the notions of 'instinct' and 'archetype', Kerslake sets himself the task of demonstrating that, in various guises, the ethological, 'somnambulist theory of instinct' profoundly preoccupied Deleuze from 1953 to 1961 and beyond (53; 91–92). One cannot help but admire in this work Kerslake's eye for detail. It does seem, however, that Kerslake at times makes too much of the sparse textual evidence available for such claims. For example, quite a bit of weight is given to the above-mentioned footnote on Jung in *Difference and Repetition*. As noted above, Kerslake effectively concludes from this 'important reference' that 'Deleuze takes up Jung's model in this theory of problematic Ideas in *Difference and Repetition*' (96). However, since this note only appears in the context of a critique of the Freudian conflictual model of the drives and of Deleuze's counter-postulation of its 'differential' basis, perhaps it would be more appropriate to the evidence to argue that Deleuze is here simply signaling with a footnote that the notion of a differential or problematic conception of the unconscious, such as he himself is developing it throughout *Difference and Repetition*, is not completely foreign to psychoanalysis.

Several other shortcomings can be identified as weakening Kerslake's claims. Firstly, in order to suggest the similarity of their ideas, Kerslake sometimes juxtaposes long analyses of Bergson, Jung or Schopenhauer, with citations from Deleuze which have been isolated from their context and which are devoid of any conceptual elaboration. The problem here is that, left in such a state of generality, Deleuze's pronouncements can do no more than 'recall' or suggest an analogy with the work of these other thinkers, rather than demonstrate, as Kerslake seems to want them to do, Deleuze's conceptual debt to them. Thus, for example, we are asked to compare a citation from Deleuze's *Expressionism in Philosophy: Spinoza* (1990b) with Kerslake's long analyses of Jung and Schopenhauer, but without any real discussion of what is at stake in *Expressionism* as a whole or in the Deleuzian concept of 'expression' which is, moreover, the focus of the citation (151). Or again, after a long analysis of Jung, when Kerslake claims that 'Deleuze's and Guattari's theory that desire must be articulated in terms of intensities is not so far from the Jungian theory of psychic energy', the ensuing brief discussion of several references to *Anti-Oedipus* (not one of which mentions the concept of 'intensity') does not seem enough to justify the conclusion that Deleuze never really left behind 'the most fundamental Jungian principles' (74).

It also detracts from Kerslake's arguments that he sometimes does not clearly distinguish 'who' is speaking in the Deleuzian texts that he analyses, about 'what' and with what problem or aim in mind. This is particularly apparent when Kerslake all but identifies Deleuze's own views with his editorial 'selection' for *Instincts and Institutions*, when he treats the text of Deleuze's foreword to Jean Malfatti's *Études sur la Mathèse ou Anarchie et Hiérarchie de la Science* (1946) as the expression of a youthful Deleuze's own thought, and, finally, when he examines the essay, 'De Sacher-Masoch au masochisme'. While it is true that Deleuze's own ideas and interests permeate his work on other thinkers, this does not authorise the assimilation of Deleuze's thought with the particular figure under consideration in this or that Deleuzian text: that is, at least, not without asking what is at stake in that particular engagement. Thus, for example, it seems too hasty to claim that in 'De Sacher-Masoch au masochisme' Deleuze 'seems to endorse a Jungian, epochal view of history, with Anima and Animus as the main protagonists' (77), particularly when we add that Deleuze's aim in this essay was to develop a psychoanalytical account of masochism which differed from the unsatisfactory Freudian model, and that he found in Jung certain conceptual tools that seemed appropriate to Sacher-Masoch's texts and, moreover, to the suggestive imagery to be found therein.[2]

Finally, it would have strengthened Kerslake's 'genealogy' of Deleuze's views on the unconscious if, in his discussion of Deleuze's introduction to Malfatti, he had tried to establish the reasons why Deleuze retracted his acknowledgement of this text. Kerslake writes that it 'is not an *a priori* mistake to take a philosophical text written by a twenty-one-year-old seriously' (213, n.23). This is, of course, quite true. But without an account of *why* Deleuze might have disowned this text, it is difficult to see the *continuity* between this early work and Deleuze's later writings. The terminological coincidences between Malfatti's and Deleuze's work that Kerslake notes in order to bolster his argument do not suffice for this task, since, in the absence of further analysis and elaboration, terminological coincidences do not automatically make for conceptual coincidences:

> [O]ccult themes run throughout Deleuze's work: not only does the term 'mathesis' appear at crucial points of *Difference and Repetition*, along with a weird emphasis on the esoteric use of the mathematical calculus, but his interest in somnambulism, the notion of the world as an egg, the theory of the second birth and the recurring image of the hermaphrodite all refer back to ideas found in Malfatti's book. (125)[3]

Kerslake's book is thus, in short, a very promising, if ultimately unsatisfying attempt at establishing Deleuze's relationship to certain esoteric notions of the unconscious. Kerslake's painstaking research has, however, garnered a wealth of historical and bibliographical information which will be of great interest to Deleuzian scholars.

Sean Bowden
The University of New South Wales & L'Université de Paris VIII,
Vincennes – Saint-Denis
DOI: 10.3366/E1750224108000421

References

Deleuze, Gilles (1946) 'Mathèse, Science et Philosophie', introduction to Jean Malfatti de Montereggio, *Études sur la Mathèse ou Anarchie et Hiérarchiede la Science*, Paris: Éditions du Griffon d'Or, pp. ix–xxiv
Deleuze, Gilles (ed.) (1953) *Instincts et institutions*, Paris: Hachette.
Deleuze, Gilles (1961) 'De Sacher-Masoch au masochisme', Arguments, 21, pp. 40–6.
Deleuze, Gilles (1967b) *Présentation de Sacher-Masoch*, Paris: Éditions de Minuit. Contains 'Le froid et le cruel'.
Deleuze, Gilles (1990a) *The Logic of Sense*, trans. Mark Lester with Charles Stivale, edited by Constantin Boundas, New York: Columbia University Press.
Deleuze, Gilles (1990b) *Expressionism in Philosophy: Spinoza*, New York: Zone Books.
Deleuze, Gilles (1994) *Difference and Repetition*, trans. Paul Patton, New York: Columbia University Press.
Deleuze, Gilles, (1998) 'How Do We Recognize Structuralism?' trans. M. McMahon & C. Stivale in C. Stivale, *The Two-Fold Thought of Deleuze and Guattari*, New York: Semiotext(e), pp. 251–82.
Deleuze, Gilles & Guattari, Félix (1983) *Anti-Oedipus: Capitalism and Schizophrenia*, Minneapolis: University of Minnesota Press.
Holland, Eugene (1999) *Deleuze and Gauttari's Anti-Œdipus: Introduction to Schizoanalysis*, London: Routledge.

Notes

1. To list some examples: 'Jungianism continues to shape [Deleuze's] theory of the unconscious right up to *Difference and Repetition*' (69); 'It is not clear that Deleuze ever really left behind the most fundamental Jungian principles" (74); '[H]e seems to endorse a Jungian, epochal view of history, with Anima and Animus as the main protagonists' (77); 'The notion of a "second birth", rebirth or renaissance [which has an esoteric background] is fundamental to Deleuze from the beginning' (81); '...Deleuze's attempt to ground his own Jungian notion of the symbol in Kant's aesthetics...' (105); 'In 1961, Deleuze fully affirms Jung's notion of symbolism' (111); 'In effect, Deleuze follows up the relationship between fate and the death instinct by turning to Jung's theory of synchronicity' (146); 'Deleuze thus finds a way to defend the Hermetic idea that the microcosm contains the macrocosm' (160); and the oft-found 'following Jung...', applied to Deleuze (99; 106; 151).

2. Indeed, if we base ourselves on this more cautious reading of the reference to Jung in 'De Sacher-Masoch au masochsime', it comes as less of surprise that in Deleuze's 1967 essay on Sacher-Masoch, 'Le froid et le cruel' (1967), while maintaining the same aim, Deleuze altogether drops the reference to Jung.

3. Indeed, Kerslake often makes use of these terminological coincidences in order to strengthen his general claim that that Deleuze's work is based in part on certain esoteric ideas about the unconscious. To list several of them: 'Deleuze may have come across Jung's notion of archetype while researching the theme of repetition. Not only are archetypes, apparently, impressions of ever-repeated typical experiences, but, at the same time, they behave empirically like agents that tend towards the repetition of these same experiences' [a citation from Jung's collected works]' (88); 'Jung's emphasis on the role of condensation in symbols suggests that condensation involves a different kind of synthesis, perhaps involving something like the "condensation of singularities" Deleuze discusses in relation to the determination of the Idea in *Difference and Repetition*" (109); or finally, 'The language of invisible rays runs through both magical and psychotic writings. Deleuze's appeal to the language of "flows", "intensities", "force" and "power" is rooted in that curious convergence' (173 – for further examples, see: 69–70 and 172).